Alois Mayer · Rodney Heath

ENGLISCH ABITUR
schnell trainiert

D1732533

Alois Mayer · Rodney Heath

ENGLISCH ABITUR
schnell trainiert

Für Grund- und Leistungskurse
Comprehension Tests · Word Fields · Expressing Ideas
Ausführliche Lösungsvorschläge

mvg verlag

Die Deutsche Bibliothek – CIP-Einheitsaufnahme

Mayer, Alois:
Englisch-Abitur schnell trainiert : für Grund- und Leistungskurse ;
comprehension tests, word fields, expressing ideas, ausführliche
Lösungsvorschläge / Alois Mayer ; Rodney Heath. – 3. Aufl. –
München / Landsberg am Lech : mvg-verl., 1992
  (mvg-Lernhilfen)
  ISBN 3-478-04491-X

3. Auflage 1992

Graphiken: Gerd Heller, Pestenacker

Umschlaggestaltung: Gruber & König, Augsburg
Druck- und Bindearbeiten: WB-Druck, Rieden
Printed in Germany 040 491/992402
ISBN 3-478-04491-X

Vorwort

Englisch – Neue Comprehension Tests ist eine neuartig aufbereitete Lernhilfe mit umfangreichen Übungsmaterialien zur Vertiefung der in den curricularen Lehrplänen festgelegten Lernziele für den Grund- und Leistungskurs Englisch.

Die Abschnitte "word fields" und "expressing ideas" sind als Schwerpunkte besonders hervorzuheben: Sie enthalten grundlegendes und themenspezifisches Sprachmaterial, aus dem Sie in zweifacher Hinsicht gewinnen können:

a) Sie erweitern Ihren Wortschatz zu aktuellen Themenbereichen ("word fields") und vergrößern Ihr allgemeines Textverständnis (passive Kenntnisse).

b) Sie eignen sich verschiedene, sprachlich variierende Wendungen an: Dadurch werden Sie in Ihrer Ausdrucksfähigkeit flexibler (aktive Kenntnisse), und es fällt Ihnen leichter, abstrakte Sachverhalte korrekt zu formulieren ("expressing ideas").

Zu allen Fragen zum Text finden Sie Lösungen, anhand derer Sie Ihre eigenen Bearbeitungen kontrollieren können. Die Lösungen zu den Aufgabenteilen "Composition" und "Translate" stellen Lösungsvorschläge dar.

Hinweis zur Arbeitstechnik

Im Anschluß an jeden Kapiteltext finden Sie ein dreispaltiges "Vocabulary". Versuchen Sie zunächst, die Bedeutung der einzelnen Wörter und Wendungen aus den angegebenen Definitionen und Synonymen herauszufinden, bevor Sie sich auf die deutsche Entsprechung konzentrieren. Sie üben damit für den "Ernstfall", für Schulaufgaben, Klassenarbeiten und für das Abitur, bei denen ein einsprachiges Wörterbuch als Hilfsmittel benutzt werden kann.

Die Verfasser

Anmerkung zur 3. Auflage:

Aus Gründen der Aktualität wurde der Text "A 'Chunnel' Vs. a 'Brunnel'" ersetzt durch "Britain's Race Relations".

Contents

II. Nützliche Wörter und Wendungen

Useful words and structures

(word fields – expressing ideas)

acceptance 60
advertising 132
analogy 102
arguments 60
association 84

catastrophy 35
cause 130
censorship 36
characteristic 89
cliché 87
common place 87
comparing 134, 136
comparison 136
contrary 106
contrast 107
conviction 16

death 103
decease 103
deeds 21
desire 20
developments 128
difference 135
discrimination 61
disease 103
duty – duties 62

effect 130
effort 110

energy problems 42
event 127
example 84
excitement 20

fear 23

habit 80
happen 127
hire 131
holiday 83
humourous 86

illness 103
integration 61
importance 63
(great ~)
intelligence 53
invade 79
irresponsibility 111

judge 133

knowledge 22

language 56

to match 88
mistrust 39

nuclear power 40

part of 126
(to be ~)
pollution 104

reactions 64
reproach 34
responsibility 111
right – rights 62

sameness 135
segregation 61
similarity 135
skill 129
space 17
stress 108
(to ~)

trust 38

usefulness 19
(utility) 19
uselessness (19)
(inutility) 19

9

III. Stylistic devices (rhetorical figures) – Stilmittel·

IV. Grammar

V. Word formation

1. Still worth it

On Tuesday, Jan. 28, 1986, the space shuttle 'Challenger' exploded a few minutes after its lift-off. The crew, six astronauts and a woman teacher, were killed. This was the worst accident in the history of space exploration.

The fireball that snuffed out seven strong young lives above Cape Canaveral will not end America's tryst with space. The space age is only just beginning. It is 25 years – an eye's blink – since the first orbit in space by a man. Yet space has already become far too important for
5 earthlings to abandon.

It matters for two different sorts of reasons. Grand ones, which have to do with enlarging the human spirit and discovering new worlds. And practical ones, which concern the condition of ordinary people on earth. Spacecraft can deliver men to the moon and count the rings on
10 Saturn. They can also give warning of storms, beam subversive soap operas into the backyards of tyrants, prospect for minerals, help prevent wars and make it easier to telephone granny.

It is because there are two big themes in space – the noble and the prosaic – that space programmes in democratic countries are controver-
15 sial. It is difficult for poets or politicians to strike the right balance between them. America spent $25 billion (in 1968-dollars) so that Neil Armstrong could make his giant leap for mankind – a leap that brought little glee to scientists or accountants. But citizens still throng the Air and Space Museum in Washington to touch briefly the odd
20 fragment of stone that Apollo brought back from the moon.

Although many of the jobs of astronauts could be done by robots, taxpayers will not support a space programme that denies them all the thrilling spectacle of human beings cavorting in weightlessness or drifting on slender tethers far above a distant earth. And if some of these
25 human beings are chosen as symbols, as they have been, why deny the value of symbolism? In space, as on earth, there will always be some jobs that only human beings can do.

Those who say, with hindsight, that the dangers of all manned

spaceflight far outweigh the benefits are wrong. Circumstances con-
30 spired to make the explosion that destroyed *Challenger* peculiarly
poignant. It was utterly unexpected: 24 successful flights had made the
shuttle look routine. It happened while Mrs. Christa McAuliffe, a
teacher and America's first ordinary civilian in space, was on board.
And it happened on television, so that millions could see the explosion
35 and the grief of the watching families.

Despite this triple shock, the exploration of space has so far been safer
than anybody had a right to expect. Since 1961, when Yuri Gagarin
flew into orbit, fewer than 20 people have died on board spacecraft.
Astronauts know that they are exposing themselves to special risks.
40 Like test pilots, many of whom died in aircraft's pioneering days, they
do their job gladly in spite of the risk, and sometimes because of it.

To say that accidents will happen and to press on regardless is, of
course, not enough. The National Aeronautics and Space Administration (NASA) had only four space shuttles. The loss of *Challenger* and
45 the grounding of the other three is a heavy blow, not only to America's
space programme, but also to the plans of allies who had booked shuttles to launch their own satellites and planetary expeditions. Even if
shuttle flights start again soon, many missions − military, commercial
and scientific − will be cancelled or postponed. It would be foolish if
50 America did not pause to take stock of its priorities in space.

The shuttle, but not the station

In doing so it should not become obsessed with asking whether space
should be explored by men or machines. The answer is obvious: by
both. The seven deaths will not deflect America from manned
spaceflight after it has already invested $25 billion in today's dollars
55 − and so much justified pride − in building the shuttle. The issue is
not whether man belongs in space but whether he is doing the right
things there.

Many people think he is not. In particular, President Reagan's decision
in 1984 to make the development of the space station into the cen-
60 trepiece of the West's space programme throughout the 1990s was

12

unimaginative. A permanently-manned hotel parked above the earth does not seem useful enough to justify the expense. To be sure, there is a chance – a remote one – that man will one day make useful things in space that cannot be made on the gravity-polluted earth. But, for
65 some years to come, this possibility can be explored less grandly on the shuttle.

America's first priority after the trauma of *Challenger* should be to rehabilitate the shuttle. Its second should be to draw up a bold new plan for the exploration of space, using manned spacecraft to visit
70 Mars and unmanned robots to go beyond. In this of all weeks, the future still beckons.

I. Vocabulary

to snuff out	to put an end to, to extinguish	auslöschen
a tryst (old use)	an appointment between lovers to meet at a secret time or place	Verabredung, Rendezvous, Stelldichein
orbit	the path of a man-made object round the earth	Umlaufbahn, Kreisbahn
an earthling (lit) (often found in science fiction)	used for a human being by a creature from another world	Erdenbewohner
to beam to/into	(of radio waves) to send out in a certain direction	ausstrahlen
soap opera	a daily or weekly continuing television or radio story, which is usually about the characters' private troubles	rührselige Hörspiel- oder Fernsehserie (Anm.: früher oft von Seifenfirmen zu Werbezwecken finanziert)
granny (infml)	grandmother	Oma
glee	a feeling of joyful satisfaction at sth. which pleases one	Freude, Heiterkeit, Fröhlichkeit

to throng	to move as if in a crowd	sich scharen, sich drängen
to cavort	to jump or dance about	herumhüpfen
a tether	a rope or chain to which an animal is tied	Leine, Halteseil
hindsight	the ability to see how and why something happened, especially to know that it could have been prevented	(zu späte) Einsicht
to press on	to advance with courage or without delay	weitermachen
to ground	here: to cause a pilot or a plane to stay on the ground	Startverbot erteilen
to take stock of	to consider the state of things so as to take a decision	erwägen, überlegen
to deflect from	(to cause) to turn from a straight course of direction	abbringen, ablenken, abweichen
to beckon	to make a silent sign (as with the fingers) to call someone	herbeiwinken, -locken, -rufen

Pitfalls in the language

1. space – unbegrenzter Raum, Weltraum
   – begrenzter Raum (a parking space – Parkplatz)
   spacious – geräumig
   spatial – (techn. Begriff) räumlich

2. to discover – (etwas Neues) entdecken
   to explore – (etwas bereits Bekanntes) erforschen

3. Zivil**ist** = civil**ian**

Note on a stylistic figure in syntax: **ellipsis**

(It is) Still worth it.

In the title, the author uses an ellipsis, i.e. the leaving out of one or more words from a sentence when the meaning can be understood without them.

An ellipsis is often used **to avoid repetition**.

Ellipsis is characteristic of **familiar** spoken language.

Examples: (I) Beg your pardon.
(Do you) Want a drink?
(It is) Nice to see you.
(I'll) See you later.

II. Questions on the text

1. Explain the author's conviction as expressed in the first paragraph of the article. (See p. 16)

2. In what way will the exploration of space contribute to "enlarge the human spirit"? (Line 7) (See p. 17)

3. Comment on the practical reasons that speak for continuing space flights. (Line 12: "They can also give . . . to telephone granny.") (See p. 18)

4. In line 21 to 24 the author states a behaviour that is typical of man. Analyse it. (See p. 20)

5. What are astronauts a symbol of? (See p. 21)

6. For what reasons does the author advocate the carrying on of space flights?
(Pay special attention to "listing" the arguments.) (See p. 22)

7. A growing number of people are concerned about the military purpose of space flights. Describe their concern. (See p. 22)

8. Summarize the last three paragraphs. (See p. 23)

9. Composition: The United States has repeatedly invited Western European states to collaborate with it on space programmes. For what reasons should Western Europe accept this inivitation? (See p. 24)

10. Translate (See p. 24)

1. Explain the author's conviction as expressed in the first paragraph of the text.

The author firmly believes that it is America's intention to continue the exploration of space despite the 'Challenger' disaster. The death of the seven people, killed when being launched into space, will not prevent further space flights.

Expressing ideas: conviction − Überzeugung

Someone is	convinced that . . .	− *überzeugt, daß . . .*
	assured that . . .	− *sicher, daß . . .*
	confident that . . .	− *zuversichtlich, daß . . .*
	persuaded that . . .	− *überzeugt, daß . . .*

| Someone is | firmly / thoroughly } − *fest* | convinced that . . . |

| A convincing / compelling | − *überzeugendes* / − *zwingendes* | argument |

(to speak) from conviction − *. . . aus Überzeugung*
a convinced supporter of . . . − *ein überzeugter Anhänger von . . .*

| to persuade someone **of** | −*jemanden überzeugen von . . .* |
| to persuade someone **into** | −*jemanden überreden zu . . .* |

16

Word field: space — Weltraum

space shuttle — *Raumfähre*   spacecraft ⎫ — *Raumschiff*
                                      spaceship ⎭

manned/unmanned space flight   — *bemannter/unbemannter Weltraumflug*

space age   — *das Zeitalter der Weltraumfahrt*
space mission   — *Auftrag im Weltraum*
space research   — *Weltraumforschung*

arms race in space   — *Wettrüsten im All*
demilitarization of space — *Entmilitarisierung des Weltraums*

to lift a spacecraft into orbit   — *ein Raumschiff auf eine Umlaufbahn bringen*

2. In what way will the exploration of space contribute to "enlarge the human spirit"? (Line 7)

Exploring the universe man will learn more about the world he lives in and about himself, especially about his origin. He will discover new principles and the natural laws all existence is subject to. This may eventually lead to a better understanding of his own life.

Pitfalls: human — 1. menschlich, 2. menschenfreundlich
          humane — human, menschenfreundlich

mankind/humanity   — Menschheit
human being   — (der einzelne) Mensch
the humanities   — Studium der antiken Kultur (Sprache, Literatur, usw.)

3. Comment on the practical reasons that speak for continuing space flights. (Line 12 "They can also give . . . to telephone granny.")

With the knowledge won from space flights, satellites can be launched which can better measure and help predict weather conditions. This is particularly important for ships and airplanes. If they are informed in time of an approaching storm measures can be taken so as not to endanger passengers' lives.

Tyrants or despotic governments need to isolate their people from all information coming from countries with a freer form of government in order to secure their rules. It is, however, hardly possible to prevent radio or TV programmes, transmitted by satellites. Through these programmes, the people under their yoke will learn about the standards of living, or the greater liberties in other, more democratic countries. This awareness will make them dissatisfied with their conditions and may lead them to undermine and finally overthrow the tyrant's rule.

In our increasingly industrialized world, there is a rising demand for natural resources. They will soon be exhausted and there is an urgent need to discover new ones. Satellites can facilitate this search, for example by detecting minerals under the polar icecaps.

Political tensions between nations may lead to wars. Before a nation is ready to begin a war, she will make preparations, such as gathering troops at the borders, experimenting with new weapons, or if the worst comes to the worst carrying out atomic tests. These preparations will not escape the attention of a satellite stationed in space and surveying critical areas, and countermeasures, for example negotiations to settle problems peacefully, can be taken.

Lastly, satellites can improve communications, be it by facilitating international telephone calls or by transmitting information effectively in other ways.

Expressing ideas: a) usefulness, utility – Nützlichkeit

| A satellite, space research, etc. | facilitates
betters
improves
enables us to | – *erleichtert*
– *verbessert*
– *ermöglicht es uns* | to do sth. |

| Something is | useful
of use
of service
expedient | – *nützlich* | for doing sth. |

| Something is helpful for the purpose of | something
doing something |

Something suits one's purpose – *Etwas eignet sich (gut) für einen Zweck*

b) uselessness, inutility – Nutzlosigkeit

| The | worthlessness
unemployability
insufficiency
inefficiency | – *Wertlosigkeit*
– *Unbrauchbarkeit*
– *Untauglichkeit*
– *Unwirksamkeit* | of . . . |

| Something is | lost labour.
in vain.
a waste of time/money. | – *. . . vergebliche Mühe.*
– *. . . vergeblich.*
– *. . . Zeit-/Geld-verschwendung.* |

It is no use **doing** (sth.). – *Es hat keinen Sinn/Wert (etwas zu tun).*

4. In line 21 to 24 the author states a behaviour that is typical of man. Analyse it.

Man seems to be very eager to watch sensational spectacles, his fellow beings risk their lives. Apart from the area of space travels, this excited interest can also be observed when people attend car races or when they are spectators of the hazardous (1) feats of artists in a circus show. Man is willing to pay a more or less considerable amount of money to satisfy his sensationalism (2).

(1) hazardous   – gewagt, lebensgefährlich
(2) sensationalism   – Sensationsgier, -sucht

Word field: a) desire – Wunsch, Verlangen, Begehren, Lust, Sehnsucht

---

Man | longs
     | craves | for   }   – *sehnt sich nach*
     | yearns

Man is | eager to do sth.
         | keen on doing sth. }   – *begierig, erpicht auf*
         | unable to resist doing sth.   – *kann nicht widerstehen*

---

b) excitement – Erregung, Aufregung

People are | electrified   – *. . . wie elektrisiert . . .*
           | stirred   by . . .   – *erregt, (tief) bewegt*
           | thrilled   watching the   – *erschüttert, ergriffen*
           | stunned   astronauts,   – *verblüfft*
           | overwhelmed   etc.   } – *überwältigt*
           | overpowered

c) deeds – (große) Taten

People are impressed by the
- performance, achievement } – *Leistung*
- exploits, feats } – *Heldentaten*
- prowess, bravery } – *Tapferkeit*

of . . .

This is a
- audacious, brave, bold } – *kühn, mutig*
- spirited – *beherzt*

deed.

Neil Armstrong's landing on the moon **has made history**.

5. What are astronauts a symbol of?

Astronauts symbolically represent the idea that man is superior to robots, machines or computers which are only a means to help him in his brave effort to explore space. Space technology is, of course, of great service for progress in this field, but we should not forget that it is man's intellect and prowess which are able to master it.

> Note on stylistic devices: **the symbol**
>
> Symbols are signs or concrete objects which represent persons, abstract ideas, values, etc.
>
> Examples: The fox **is a symbol of** cleverness.
> A white flag **symbolizes** surrender. (Kapitulation, Aufgabe)
> Astronauts **serve as a symbol of** human prowess.

21

6. For what reasons does the author advocate the carrying on of space flights? (Pay special attention to "listing" your arguments.)

To begin with, space flights will contribute to human knowledge and scientific progress. Moreover, everybody will profit in his daily life from the construction and stationing of space stations and satellites. Furthermore, America has already invested too much money in the exploration of space to break it off now.

In addition, up to the disaster of Challenger very few astronauts had lost their lives.

The next item is that military, commercial and scientific enterprises, in which other nations are interested as well, should not be delayed.

Lastly, America should not put her technological superiority in the field of space travel at stake (1).

(1) to put at stake – aufs Spiel setzen

Word field: knowledge – Kenntnis

Man's	knowledge of	– *Kenntnis*	nature is
	understanding **of**	– *Verständnis* **für**	incomplete.
	insight into	– *Einsicht in*	

7. A growing number of people are concerned about the "military" purpose of space flights. Describe their concern.

These people fear that military missions in space may lead to a new arms race. Up to now the superpowers have kept on inventing ever more dreadful weapons on earth. If the military aspect of space research comes to the fore, weapons will be moved from the earth's surface to space, thus posing a deadly threat to mankind.

People	fear	– *fürchten,*	an arms race
	dread	– *befürchten,*	in space.
	apprehend (fml)	– *sich fürchten vor*	

Many people build	terrified by ⎫	– *von Schrecken*	nuclear
atomic shelters	scared of ⎭	*erfüllt*	weapons.
because they are	frightened by/of	– *verängstigt wegen*	
	horrified by	– *entsetzt über*	

Satellites used for	a dreadful ⎫	– *angsteinflößend*	prospect.
military aims are	a fearful ⎭		

Some politicians think that

weapons in space	– *Weltraumwaffen*
long range missiles	– *Langstreckenraketen*
a space arsenal	– *ein Waffenlager im Weltall*
nuclear warheads	– *nukleare Sprengköpfe*

is/are a key to world peace.

8. Summarize the last three paragraphs.

It is obvious that both man and machines should explore space. Despite the Challenger setback, Americans ought to be proud of their space programme and continue to spend money on it. President Reagan's idea of a manned space station does not appear to be the right plan for the near future, whereas a continuation of the shuttle project does. America's main aim should be to maintain the shuttle, but space exploration should also be diversified to include manned trips to Mars and unmanned ones beyond.

9. Composition.

The United States has repeatedly invited Western Europe to collaborate with it on space programmes. For what reasons should Western Europe accept this invitation?

European participation in America's space programme is essential firstly because of the latter's technological lead in this field; through collaboration the Europeans will be able to profit from the Americans' knowledge and eventually make up lost technological ground. From a financial point of view, too, it would be wise for the Europeans to learn from the greater experience of the Americans. Europe has the opportunity of exploiting already existing rockets and other facilities that would be too costly for them to develop on their own.

The economic aspect of space research cannot be ignored. Through its space programme the United States has been able to improve a wide range of materials and manufactured goods from teflon frypans to computer equipment. For Europeans to face this competition and keep their market share they must participate in space research as well. All in all, it is imperative that Europe not fall behind the USA in this most important field of human endeavour. The Americans are already moving towards a firm monopoly in space research in the Western World and if the Europeans ignore the opportunities for competition open to them, they might just miss the boat (1) altogether.

(1) to miss the boat – den Anschluß verpassen

10. Translate.

To Man or Not to Man?

The best of times, the worst of times for America's space program: just days after the unmanned Voyager 2 spacecraft reached the planet Uranus – only one minute off the time planned five full years ago – the shuttle Challenger exploded. It was a jarring coincidence and reopened a debate in the space-science community: must men and women probe the universe in person or can they send technological proxies?

The origins of the debate lie in the early 1970s, when NASA proposed launching satellites from reusable, manned vehicles rather than expendable rockets. It would be cheaper, NASA officials argued. The agency also stressed the sort of functions that only humans can perform, such as building the space station it hopes to orbit by the early 1990s. The station would probably be constructed of prefabricated sections assembled by humans; it would then require a permanent contingent of six to eight men and women to perform such tasks as servicing and refuelling satellites.

Vocabulary

to jar	not to go well together, to contrast unpleasantly	nicht harmonieren mit, in Gegensatz stehen zu
coincidence	events happening at the same time	(Zufall,) Zusammentreffen
a proxy	a person whom one chooses to act for one	Stellvertreter
reusable	that can be used again	wiederverwendbar
expendable	that may be used up for a purpose	1. entbehrlich 2. (nur) einmal verwendbar

Bemannte oder unbemannte Raumschiffahrt?

Auf dem Höhepunkt des amerikanischen Weltraumprogramms ereignete sich zugleich sein schlimmster Tiefpunkt: Nur einige Tage, nachdem das unbemannte Raumschiff Voyager 2 den Planeten Uranus erreicht hatte, und das mit nur einer Minute Abweichung vom Zeitplan, der vor fünf Jahren erstellt worden war, explodierte die Raumfähre Challenger. Das Zusammentreffen dieser beiden Ereignisse war ein schriller Mißton, der den Streit der an der Erforschung des Weltraums beteiligten Länder von neuem belebte: Müssen es unbedingt Männer und Frauen sein, die das Universum erkunden, oder kann man an ihrer Stelle Maschinen einsetzen?

Diese Streitfrage geht zurück auf die frühen siebziger Jahre, als die NASA den Vorschlag machte, Satelliten lieber von wiederverwendbaren, bemannten Raumschiffen aus zu starten, als sie mit nur einmal verwendbaren Raketen im All auszusetzen. Die Weltraumbehörde hob auch jene Art von Aufgaben hervor, die nur Menschen ausführen können, zum Beispiel den Bau einer Weltraumstation, die, wie die Behörde hofft, in den frühen neunziger Jahren in eine Umlaufbahn gebracht werden kann. Wahrscheinlich würde die Weltraumstation aus vorfabrizierten Teilen von Menschen zusammengesetzt werden; es wäre dann notwendig, daß sich dort ständig eine Mannschaft von sechs oder sieben Frauen und Männern aufhält, um Aufgaben wie zum Beispiel die Wartung der Satelliten oder die Treibstoffversorgung auszuführen.

Polish up your grammar

The use of "will"

The auxiliary **will** expresses:

1. Futurity in all persons. (For "shall" see p. 91.)

2. Assumption (Annahme, Vermutung)
   It **will** be necessary to improve safety regulations.

3. Polite requests
   Will you please help me.

4. Willingness
   I **will** be delighted to help you.

5. Insistence (Beharren, Bestehen auf)
   NASA **will** continue its programme despite heavy criticism.

6. Prediction (Vorhersage)
   Accidents **will** happen.

7. Habits and characteristics
   He **will** read for hours.

8. Intention

   They **will** carry it out, come what may.

Note on translating: It is often necessary to pay special attention to the different meanings of "will".

Examples: 2. Assumption   Es ist **wahrscheinlich/vermutlich** notwendig . . .

            6. Prediction   Unfälle wird es **immer** geben.

            7. Habit   **Gewöhnlich** liest er stundenlang.

2. The Chernobyl Syndrome
Twilight of the Nuclear God

Man should surely have learned by now to be respectful of new technology. The nuclear accident that sent a deadly cloud of radioactive particles roaming over Europe last week was bound to happen: the only worthwhile questions were when and where. We now know the
5 answers – at Chernobyl, in the Ukraine, on or about 26 April 1986.

There were, it is true, some special circumstances. The Chernobyl reactor would not have been licensed as safe for use today in any Western country. And the anxieties about the possible consequences of the accident were fuelled by the refusal of the Soviet authorities to say clearly
10 what had happened and what they were doing about it. We still do not know the total release of radioactivity, nor the sequence of events that precipitated it.

But sooner or later, special circumstances notwithstanding, a Chernobyl disaster was inevitable. The world has been waiting for it since
15 the Three Mile Island plant in Pennsylvania almost blew up seven years ago. Most people recognize intuitively what seems impossible for many engineers to admit: all machines have the capacity to fail, and complex machines do so in ways their designers did not anticipate. In this the public is wiser than those who persist in saying, as the chairman of the
20 Central electricity Generating Board did last week, that "it cannot happen here". It can, and – given sufficient time – it probably will. It already has, admittedly on a less alarming scale, at the Windscale plant in 1957.

It would be more truthful, as well as demonstrating some grasp of
25 history, if Ministers and other spokesmen for the nuclear industry were to recognize that disasters not only occur, but actually represent the steps by which a technology is assimilated into the world. During the nineteenth century it was the explosions of steam boilers, the collapse of bridges and the failures of signalling systems which finally pro-
30 duced the safest form of transport yet developed – the railways. In our own time, air travel has been punctuated by disasters from which

lessons have been learned. The recent explosion of the space shuttle Challenger is a textbook example of the humiliation that awaits those who claim technology is infallible. Without straining for paradox, one
35 can argue that the history of technology is a history of disasters, each leading to better and safer machines.

Why cannot the same be true of nuclear power? First, because the experts (as well as Ministers of the Crown who ought to know better) insist on declaring that accidents cannot happen, even when one just has.
40 Second, because the impact of a nuclear accident is potentially so huge that the world can hardly afford the cost of learning from its own mistakes. A Chernobyl here might have devastated half of England and Wales; a Chernobyl in France, with the wind in the right direction, might also have devastated half of England and Wales. Even if one
45 shares some politicians' cosy certainties, one cannot control what might happen elsewhere, and radioactive clouds recognize no international boundaries.

The truth is that nuclear fission has always been an uncomfortable technology, promising a long-lived and economical source of energy,
50 but demanding in return ceaseless vigilance over the power stations and their waste products. Developed and open societies like those of the West may get the better of this bargain with the devil, possessing the right combination of professional discipline and democratic institutions to control the technology while preventing any dangerous abuses
55 of it. The Three Mile Island* accident shook this conviction without wholly destroying it.

But it has never seemed sensible to imagine a world of 160 sovereign States with nuclear power stations dotted about at random. Chernobyl has shown how an authoritarian government can impose unacceptable
60 dangers on its people, in this case apparently because the type of reactor that failed is a good producer of the plutonium needed for nuclear weapons. But the Soviet Union is not unique in this respect. Many other governments at least as authoritarian, but lacking the depth of Soviet technical expertise, would be likely to make an even greater
65 mess.

To pursue the argument further, it is significant that the Western country with the most open society of all, the United States, has effectively abandoned nuclear power. Since the Three Mile Island accident* there have been no new orders, and many cancellations. Among the Western
70 countries it is Britain and France, with their nationalized electricity utilities, who remain almost the last redoubt of nuclear optimism.

This would be more understandable if there were any pressing need for new power stations. The economic arguments have faded with the decline of the oil price and the success of energy conservation.

75 Chernobyl has been a disaster out of which little credit can be discerned. If the Soviet Government maintains its traditional contempt for the open exchange of information, we may never know how many people have suffered and died as a result of it. But it will have had some benefits if it finally convinces the doubters that nuclear power has no
80 long-term future.

* Note: Three Mile Island Plant

It was the worst accident in a U.S. nuclear power plant due to equipment failure and human errors in 1979. Only 45 minutes before a catastrophe, the plant was able to be shut down.

I. Vocabulary

| syndrome | any pattern of qualities, happenings, etc. typical of general conditions | Syndrom (aus verschiedenen Anzeichen zusammengefaßte Erscheinung oder Krankheitsbild) |

to fuel	to take in fuel, e.g. petrol	tanken
	here: causing to increase anger, fear or any strong feeling	steigern, erhöhen, Nahrung geben
to anticipate	here: to expect, to see what will happen	voraussehen
a grasp of	here: understanding	Verständnis für
to be punctuated by	to be interrupted by	unterbrochen sein, gezeichnet sein
to strain for	here: to exaggerate	übertreiben
impact	the force of an idea, system, etc.	Wirkung auf
cosy	here: naive, simple	naiv, einfältig
at random	without any plan	zufällig, willkürlich, aufs Geratewohl
utility	1. (degree of) usefulness	Nutzen
	2. here: any useful service for the public	Versorgungsbetrieb
redoubt	a small fort, forming part of a larger system of defences	Schanze, Bollwerk, Kasematte

Pitfalls in the vocabulary

1. to fail   – mißlingen, fehlschlagen, scheitern

   failure   – Fehlschlag, Mißerfolg

   failing   – Fehler, Unvollkommenheit, Schwäche

   fallible   – fehlbar

   infallible   – unfehlbar

   (line 34)

2. to anticipate   – 1. vorwegnehmen

   (line 18)   2. voraussehen

3. to recognize   – 1. **wieder**erkennen (I didn't recognize John in the photo.)

   (line 46)   2. **an**erkennen (The rebels refuse to recognize the new government.)

II. Questions

1. What does the author reproach the Soviet leaders for after the disaster of Chernobyl? (See p. 34)

2. Briefly describe the information policy of totalitarian states. (See p. 35)

3. a)What does the author reproach British politicians for supporting nuclear power plants? (See p. 36)

   b)Analyse the use of the word »certainties« in this context (line 45). (See p. 36)

4. In 1986, two technological catastrophes occurred: the explosion of the space shuttle "Challenger" and the emission of radioactivity at Chernobyl.
   Analyse the different effects of these two disasters on the public opinion as regards scientists and highly complicated technology. (See p. 37)

5. What are the dangers of radioactive contamination? (See p.39)

6. Explain the expression "a bargain with the devil" (line 52) in connection with the production of nuclear energy. (See p. 40)

7. a) What reasons does the author quote which make new nuclear power stations superfluous? (See p. 41)
   b) What other sources of energy may replace nuclear energy in the future? (Describe each in one or two sentences.) (See p. 41)

8. Summarize the 6th and the 7th paragraphs.
   "The truth is . . . − . . . an even greater mess". (See p. 42)

9. Composition: State the pros and cons of nuclear energy. (See p. 43)

10. Translate. (See p. 43)

1. What does the author reproach the Soviet leaders for after the disaster of Chernobyl?

The author blames the Soviet leaders for not only operating an unsafe reactor, but also for not having informed the countries affected by the disastrous accident at Chernobyl. In the first few days after the meltdown at the nuclear plant scientists in Western European countries measured a dangerous level of radioactivity; they did not know, however, where it came from, nor were they informed about the cause and the dimensions of the catastrophe. Thus it was difficult to take countermeasures to prevent people from being contaminated. Moreover, peoples' fears increased considerably since they ignored what was being done by the Soviet authorities to bring radiation under control.

Expressing ideas: to reproach − vorwerfen

The affected countries	blame reproach accuse	the authorities	**for** **for** **of**	not in- (*beschuldigen*) forming (*vorwerfen*) them. (*anklagen*)

to lay/put the blame **for** something **on** someone − *jemandem die Schuld geben an etwas*

This policy, etc. is	a reproach to . . . blameworthy. to be blamed for . . .	− *Diese Politik ist eine Schande für* − . . . *tadelnswert.* − . . . *Schuld an . . .*

Word field: catastrophe — Katastrophe

---

disaster — *Unglück, Verderben, Katastrophe*
adj. disastrous

calamity — *Unglück, Elend*
adj. calamitous

catastrophe — *Katastrophe, Schicksalsschlag*
adj. catastrophic
adv. catastrophi**cally**

2. Briefly describe the information policy of totalitarian states.

In totalitarian states all power is vested in the government the members of which come from only one political party. This government decides what is best for the people. In the case of information policy this means that the people are only informed about the achievements of the government — failures, catastrophes, etc., are not made publicly known, so that the government can save face.

All information for the people is censored, thus the mass media present news in a one-sided way; failures of the government are covered up. This policy, typical of a closed political system, includes the fact that the people in these states have no access to foreign newspapers, films, etc., which might criticize their government.

Expressing ideas: censorship – Zensur

Information was	held back.	– ... *geheimgehalten.*
about	censored.	– ... *zensiert.*
Chernobyl	covered up.	– ... *vertuscht, verheimlicht.*
	suppressed.	– ... *unterdrückt.*
	concealed.	– ... *verheimlicht.*

In totalitarian states there is/are	no free press.
	no independent sources of information.
	no free flow of information.
	censorship.
	political control of the mass media.

3. a) What does the author reproach British politicians for supporting nuclear power plants?
   b) Analyse the use of the word "certainties" (line 45) in this context.

a) The author's severe criticism is aimed at politicians who deny the risk of a nuclear catastrophe. He blames them for not realizing that all technological progress has been closely tied up with disasters, and he presents several examples to support his criticism.

b) The author states the politicians' "certainties" that an accident like that at Chernobyl will not happen in the Western countries. From the context, however, it becomes clear that the author is not at all convinced of what the politicians say; he is of the opinion that accidents of this sort are inevitable. The author uses "certainties" with the intention of expressing the opposite idea, namely that what politicians declare as certain is actually very "uncertain"«. He employs the word "certainties" in an ironical way.

36

Note on stylistic devices: irony

Irony is the use of words which are clearly opposite to what is meant.

Examples: It has been raining for days. That's really **beautiful** weather.
Politicians often make **wise** decisions which later on turn out to be unreasonable.

The stylistic device of **irony** is mainly used to express humour, criticism or (slight) sarcasm.

The author describes	this behaviour this attitude etc.	ironically. in a tone of irony.
The author makes an ironical	remark statement	about . . .
This ironical statement	aims at is directed against ridicules emphasizes criticizes	foolish, wrong, etc., behaviour.

4. In 1986, two technological catastrophes occurred: the explosion of the space shuttle "Challenger" and the emission of radioactivity at Chernobyl. Analyse the different effects of these two disasters on the public opinion as regards scientists and highly complicated technology.

Due to these two recent calamities one can discern three main attitudes towards scientists and technology: to begin with, a lot of people are of the opinion that scientific enterprises must go on for the benefit of mankind. They have faith in scientists and they place trust in their capacity to master all technological difficulties.

A second group supports the opposite, namely an absolute stop to all scientific activities in the fields of space research and nuclear power stations on the grounds that man is not yet able to cope with the dangers of complicated technology.

A growing number of people, especially those who previously placed full reliance on the expertise of scientists are beginning to be less trustful. They do not altogether reject scientific technology. They are, however, sceptical of the scientists' and technicians' ability to deal with these problems.

Word field: a) to trust — vertrauen

---

to trust someone to have faith **in** someone	— *jemandem vertrauen*
to rely on someone	— *sich auf jemanden verlassen*
to place trust **in** something to place reliance **on** something They place trust in the government.	— *auf etwas vertrauen*
to trust someone to do something I trust him to help me.	— *jemandem vertrauen, daß er etwas tut*
to swear by Whenever he has got a cold, he swears by whisky.	— *auf etwas schwören*
trustworthy	— *vertrauenswürdig*
trustful	— *vertrauensvoll*
to be beyond doubt	— *außer Zweifel sein*

b) to mistrust — mißtrauen

to mistrust to distrust	someone/something	*— jemandem/etwas mißtrauen*
to suspect		*— argwöhnen, Mißtrauen hegen*

the mistrust **of** something	*— Mißtrauen **an** etwas*
to be open to doubt	*— etwas muß/kann bezweifelt werden*
doubt	*— Mißtrauen, Argwohn, Zweifel*

distrustful/mistrustful	*— mißtrauisch*
sceptical of/about	*— skeptisch gegenüber*

5. What are the dangers of radioactive contamination?

The worst danger of radiation is cancer. It will kill not only people who were exposed to radiation, but also people who eat contaminated food or breathe contaminated air. There are only few possibilities to protect people from contamination, since the wind carries the deadly rays everywhere. An additional difficulty in the fight against radioactivity is the fact that in many cases the deadly effects only appear long after the contamination.

Up to the present time, science, especially medical science, has discovered no remedy for the harmful effects of radiation. Mankind is exposed to this deadly menace as helplessly as it was to the Black Death in the Middle Ages.

No nuclear power plant			absolutely safe.
The risk of nuclear accidents	is		high.
A radioactive accident			uncontrollable.

People	exposed to	radio-	will	die from cancer.
	receiving a dose of	activity		suffer from leukemia,
	contaminated by			tumors, etc.

Nuclear	a reliable	– *zuverlässig*	source of
power is	an inexhaustible	– *unerschöpflich*	electric energy.
	a long-term	– *auf lange Zeit*	
	an economical	– *wirtschaftlich*	

Antinuclear	all nuclear	be shut down.
activists	power stations	be done away with.
demand that	should	be abolished.

Some	to forego	– *verzichten auf*	nuclear
countries	to abandon	– *aufgeben*	power
have	to phase out	– *langsam aussteigen aus*	altogether.
chosen			

6. Explain the expression "a bargain with the devil" (line 52) in connection with the production of nuclear energy.

This expression refers to a motive found in literature (Doctor Faustus) and in a number of fairy-tales. A human being makes a contract with the devil: he uses the supernatural powers of the devil to attain a certain aim and in turn he must give the devil his soul after his death.

The author employs this metaphor to reveal a parallel: nuclear power is helpful in that it meets the increasing demand for energy at a time when mineral fuels are nearly exhausted. On the other hand, a high price must be paid for it: in case of accidents the human toll is considerable and the consequences for the environment incalculable.

7. a) What reasons does the author quote which make new nuclear power stations superfluous?

The author presents two arguments which speak against new power stations. First, the price for oil has dropped sharply, thus ensuring energy at lower costs. Second, the use of oil itself has declined thanks to energy-saving devices, such as cars which consume less petrol.

b) What other sources of energy may replace nuclear energy in the future? (Describe each in one or two sentences.)

There are several possibilities to produce energy in other ways. Renewable energy can be produced by wind-powered turbines in windmills. Solar rays can be caught by the use of mirrors and converted into energy which can be used to heat water. Hydroelectric power can be won from rivers and from either the waves or the tides of the sea. None of these sources pollutes the environment, nor are the devices used to convert the energy in danger of blowing up. These energy sources are, however, not yet satisfactorily developed.

The use of oil | is indispensable for cars.
              | delivers consumers into the hands of OPEC.

Oil | is a finite, non-renewable resource.

Coal | is dangerous to mine.
     | pollutes the air.
     | produces toxic emissions.

The use of | cannot yet meet the demand for energy.
wind, | is unreliable, e.g. the sun cannot be relied on to shine.
water, | does not generate enough energy.
the sun | is costly to develop.

8. Summarize the 6th and the 7th paragraphs.
   "The truth is . . . — . . . an even greater mess."

Nuclear fission is an economical method of producing energy but also one which calls for constant vigilance. Open Western societies achieve the right balance of professional discipline and democratic institutions which ensure that the dangers and potential abuses of nuclear power are kept to a minimum. Authoritarian governments, however, often subject their countries' citizens to unnecessary risks. Thus the Soviet Union's desire to produce nuclear weapons was fulfilled at the cost of using unsafe reactors.

Other less experienced countries are able to cause even greater catastrophes than Chernobyl.

9. Composition: State the pros and cons of nuclear energy.

It is first of all important to remember that nuclear power is a relatively cheap energy source which does not involve the huge development costs of alternative energy forms. Secondly, nuclear energy fulfills our increasing energy needs when they have to be fulfilled: now it is, moreover, an essential substitute for other resources such as coal and oil which are now becoming scarce. In addition, the use of nuclear power encourages the growth of industry through the supply of cheap power. Finally, nuclear power is, on the whole, a reliable energy source.

On the other hand, the disadvantages of nuclear power cannot be overlooked. Though for the most part reliable, nuclear power plants can malfunction – with catastrophic results. Any energy form which, in unfavourable circumstances, can unleash the force of an atom bomb on the environment must surely be considered essentially dangerous. A second disadvantage of this sort of power is its prestige value, which induces countries with a low technological standard to enter this field: lack of awareness of the problems involved and low safety standards may lead to further catastrophes. A further point which speaks against the use of nuclear power is its potential abuse for military purposes: of all energy forms it is the least "peaceful". Lastly, nuclear power creates problems not only now but also in the future. The problem of how to dispose of nuclear waste is far from solved and present methods, whether subterranean or submarine, are bound to be a legacy for coming generations.

10. Translate

What odds are acceptable?

It helps little to say that technology should be made as safe as possible. Machines can almost always be made safer, but at some stage the price of the extra safety spoils the point of the machine. Cars designed to travel no faster than five miles an hour would be safe but useless: the

5 point of the contraption is to take people quickly from one place to another. America did not develop the space shuttle in order to take seven people safely into space once; the purpose of the shuttle was to take people into space regularly and cheaply.

It is easy enough, after *Challenger* and *Chernobyl*, to make scientists
10 and engineers into scapegoats. But it is the job of politicians, not scientists, to decide whether the risks associated with a new technology are acceptable or not. Scientists can try to reckon the odds, but will often get them wrong. Even if they didn't, the decisions would still be hard. Laymen find some risks more acceptable than others, for reasons that
15 have nothing to do with numbers. Risks over which they have no control − like radioactive clouds from the Ukraine − are less acceptable than bigger risks they run voluntarily by smoking, driving or rock climbing. An isolated nuclear accident that may kill many people seems worse than the thousands of car crashes that happen every month −
20 but they kill, at most, just a few at a time.

If mankind had rejected civil nuclear power as too unsafe, the world would have been spared a Chernobyl. But it would have more coal-burning and oil-burning power stations, more people killed from
25 respiratory diseases and industrial accidents, more acid rain, scarcer oil and dearer electricity. That all adds up to worse health, as well as less prosperity.

Vocabulary

odds (pl)	probability that sth. will happen	Gewinnquote hier: Risiken
contraption	(strange-looking) machine or apparatus	1. Apparat, 2. techn. Neuheit
scapegoat	person or thing taking the blame for the fault of others	Sündenbock
respiratory diseases	−	Erkrankungen der Atemwege

44

Welche Risiken sind noch tragbar?

Es hilft uns wenig, wenn wir sagen, daß die Technologie so sicher wie möglich gemacht werden sollte. Maschinen können fast immer noch sicherer gebaut werden, aber in einem bestimmten Stadium wird eine Maschine wegen der zusätzlichen Kosten für die Sicherheitsvorkehrungen wertlos. Autos, die so konstruiert sind, daß sie nicht schneller als fünf Meilen in der Stunde fahren können, wären sicher, aber nutzlos. Zweck dieser Erfindung ist, Leute rasch von einem Ort zum anderen zu befördern. Amerika hat die Raumfähre nicht entwickelt, um nur einmal sieben Menschen in den Weltraum zu befördern; es war vielmehr beabsichtigt, Menschen regelmäßig und ohne große Kosten dorthin zu bringen.

Nach den Katastrophen ''Challenger'' und ''Tschernobyl'' ist es natürlich leicht, die Wissenschaftler und Ingenieure als Sündenböcke abzustempeln. Aber es ist Aufgabe der Politiker, nicht der Wissenschaftler, darüber zu entscheiden, ob Risiken, die eine neue Technologie mit sich bringt, tragbar sind oder nicht. Wissenschaftler können versuchen, diese Risiken abzuschätzen, aber sie werden sich dabei oft irren. Selbst wenn dies nicht der Fall ist, so wäre es immer noch schwierig, Entscheidungen zu fällen. Der Laie glaubt, daß einige Risiken eher getragen werden können als andere, und dies aus Gründen, die nichts mit Zahlen zu tun haben. Risiken, die der Laie nicht kontrollieren kann, wie zum Beispiel radioaktive Wolken aus der Ukraine, sind für ihn weniger tragbar als größere, die er beim Rauchen, Autofahren oder Klettern im Fels freiwillig eingeht. Ein einzelner Unfall im Bereich der Kernenergie, bei dem viele Menschen getötet werden können, erscheint schlimmer als die Tausende von Autounfällen, die sich jeden Monat ereignen – allerdings werden dabei, wenn überhaupt, nur wenige Menschen getötet.

Hätten die Menschen die Atomenergie für zivile Zwecke abgelehnt, weil sie zu unsicher ist, so wäre ihnen ein Tschernobyl erspart geblieben. Dann aber gäbe es mehr Kraftwerke, in denen Kohle und Öl verbrannt werden, es gäbe auch mehr Todesfälle durch Erkrankung der Atemwege und Unfälle in der Industrie, mehr sauren Regen, weniger Öl und teurere Elektrizität. All das führt zu einem schlechteren Gesundheitszustand der Menschen ebenso wie zu einer Verminderung des allgemeinen Wohlstands.

Polish up your grammar

Infinitive or -ing-forms after verbs:

1. Verbs followed by the infinitive:
   . . . to do something

The politicians *determined to give up* the plan.

to agree	übereinstimmen	to instruct	unterrichten
to arrange	Anordnungen treffen	to invite	einladen
		to know	wissen
to compel	zwingen	to learn	lernen
to consent	zustimmen	to manage	gelingen
to decide	} beschließen	to order	befehlen
to determine		to refuse	ablehnen
to encourage	ermutigen	to request	bitten, fragen
to endeavour	sich bemühen	to tempt	versuchen
to hesitate	zögern	to warn	warnen

2. Verbs followed by a gerund:
   . . . doing something

He *avoided answering* my questions.

to avoid	vermeiden	to imagine	sich vorstellen
to defer	verschieben	to intend	beabsichtigen
to delay	verzögern	to mind	etw. dagegen haben
to deny	leugnen	to neglect	vernachlässigen
to dread	fürchten	to omit	unterlassen
to detest	verabscheuen	to postpone	aufschieben
to enjoy	sich erfreuen an	to prefer	vorziehen
to fancy	sich vorstellen, sich einbilden	to propose	vorschlagen
		to risk	aufs Spiel setzen
to finish	aufhören	to suspect	verdächtigen
to forgive	vergeben		

46

3. Britain's Race Relations

The subject of Britain's race relations is similar in many ways to that of England's football team or the stage of the economy. Pubs, clubs and buses are full of people who know all about what is wrong and why nothing ever seems to change for the better.

5 Consider the following assertions about what is wrong in the British racial melting pot.

- Massive post-war immigration means that non-whites make up a large part of the population.
- Non-whites have been and remain stuck in unskilled jobs because it was
10 the unskilled who left home and came to Britain in search of prosperity.
- Non-whites have higher youth unemployment levels than whites because they are poorer educational achievers and so have lower qualifications to offer.

These facts and many other with similarly wide currency are all wrong.
15 The truth ist that Britain has just over 1 m people of Asian origin and just under 1 m of Afro-Caribbean origin. This represents just four per cent of Britain's 54 m population.

Many West Indians were actively recruited through employment offices in their islands to find staff for Britain's post-war industries. A quarter of
20 the men and half the women were trained non-manual workers and a further 50 per cent of men and 25 per cent of women were skilled manual workers at the time of their arrival. White males with O-levels have an unemployment rate of 9 per cent compared with 18 per cent for Asians and 25 per cent for West Indians.

25 The various myths about newcomers are as old as immigration itself. Over the centuries Britain has accepted waves of foreigners – Jews, Huguenots, Irish, West Indians, exiled Ugandan Asians, Hong Kong Chinese and most recently, British citizens of the Asian sub-continent. Their absorption into the community has never been easy and in spite of repeat-
30 ed exposure to different races and cultures the white British, like the French, remain defensive.

But West Indians and Asians have faced two new problems in Britain: discrimination on the grounds of skin colour and a persistent racial discrimination against new British-born generations which is holding up
35 and holding back the more harmonious integration into society achieved by other immigrants. The list of discrepancies between black and white is, like the myths, endless. Widespread discrimination, illegal though it is, seems to be greatly to blame.

Detailed research by both the Home Office and the Policy Studies Insti-
40 tute suggests that non-whites are being held back through severe racial discrimination in housing, and employment and integration is further hindered by major obstacles in education and relations with the police. Lord Scarman urged that ethnic demand for under-fives nursery provision should be fully met, particularly because of the importance of ear-
45 ly tuition in language, that parents and schools must be brought closer together, that children be instructed in the way the government, institutions and the law work, and all children should leave school able to speak and write effectively in English.

The housing conditions of blacks and Asians concentrated in the inner ci-
50 ties have improved steadily over the past 20 years – principally because everybody's housing conditions have improved. So the gap remains. Even if the urgent changes needed within the education and housing systems are made now, they will take some time to percolate through. But the most immediate problems are in the employment area.

55 Home Office research shows that, again contrary to popular myth, young blacks are just as eager as whites, have the same levels of aspiration – though Asians tend to have higher aspirations than both West Indians and whites. When threatened with prolonged unemployment, the ethnic minorities have been more prepared than whites to lower their
60 sights and take a job which they would rather not have or for which they are over-qualified.

Half of non-whites, and interestingly, three quarters of whites think there are employers in Britain who would refuse a job on the grounds of race or colour, and the majority of all groups believe promotion is less
65 likely for non-whites with the same qualifications as whites.

The PSI tests show their fears to be well founded. The identical applications by letter and telephone by a white, an Asian and a West Indian were for a variety of jobs in London, Birmingham and Manchester, the three urban areas containing 60 per cent of Britain's non-white popula-
70 tion. Racial discrimination in jobs has been unlawful for 17 years, yet 25 per cent of employers discriminated against both blacks and Asians.

Proper representation throughout the ranks of the public sector would be a major counter-weight to the present levels of discrimination in employment and, if accompanied by similar efforts in schools and hous-
75 ing departments, would begin to ameliorate levels of racial discrimination which do not so far appear to have improved over the last two decades.

I. Vocabulary

assertion	forceful statement or claim	Behauptung, Versicherung
assertive	(of a person) forceful	bestimmt
melting pot	place where there is a mixing of different people, ideas, etc.	Schmelztiegel
in search of	trying to find	auf der Suche nach
prosperity	good fortune and success, especially in money matters	Wohlstand, Reichtum
to prosper	to develop favourably, to become successful and rich	blühen, gedeihen
achiever	someone who is successful especially through skill	Erfolgsmensch
currency	here: in common use or general acceptance	allgemeine Annahme, Geltung, Verbreitung
to recruit	to get someone as a new member	anwerben

staff	group of workers employed by a firm	Belegschaft, Personal
manual (workers)	using the hands	Hand-, (Handarbeiter)
O-level	(examination at) ordinary level	entspricht etwa dem Hauptschulabschluß im deutschen Schulsystem
myth	here: false story or idea	falsche Vorstellung
absorption	to make part of a community	Eingliederung, Aufnahme
exposure	here: bringing in contact	Kontakt, Gegenüberstellung
discrimination (against)	treating different people in different ways because of sex, colour, religion, etc.	Benachteiligung, Diskriminierung
persistent	continuing in a habit	beharrlich, beständig, hartnäckig
on the grounds of	because of	wegen, aufgrund
discrepancy (between)	difference	Unterschied, Verschiedenheit
to be to blame for	to be guilty of	die Schuld tragen an
to hinder from	to prevent from (being done)	(ver-)hindern an
obstacle	something which stands in the way and prevents	Hindernis
to urge	to drive or to force forward	drängen, dringend fordern
nursery	a kind of kindergarten	Kindergarten, -hort
provision	supplying of something needed	Bereitstellung, Beschaffung
to meet a demand	to satisfy what is needed	eine Forderung erfüllen
tuition	teaching, instruction	Unterricht
gap (between)	here: distance, difference	Kluft, Lücke

50

to percolate	to pass slowly through	durchsickern
promotion	advancement in rank or position	Beförderung
application	written request for a job, position	Bewerbung
proper	here: right, correct (for a purpose)	richtig, passend, geeignet
rank	here: social position	Stellung in der Gesellschaft, Rang
to ameliorate	to make better	verbessern

Pitfalls in the vocabulary

economy	– Wirtschaft, Volkswirtschaft
economics	– 1. Lehre, Wissenschaft von der Volkswirtschaft
	2. Wirtschaftspolitik, wirtschaftliche Prinzipien
economic (adj.)	– Wirtschafts-, die Wirtschaft betreffend
economical (adj.)	– sparsam, wirtschaftlich

II. Questions

1. Explain in your own words. (See p. 47, 48)
    a) Line 12   ... they are poor educational achievers...
    b) Line 14   These facts ... with (similarly) wide currency...
    c) Line 43   ...the demand for under-fives nursery provision should be fully met...

2. Analyse the stylistic device which the author uses in the second sentence of his article. (See p. 56)
3. Explain the expression "racial melting pot". (See p. 58)
4. a) Which arguments are commonly put forward to account for race problems in Britain? (See p. 59)
   b) Analyse the way in which the author counters these arguments. (See p. 59)
5. According to the text, the British and the French share the unwillingness to accept different races. What is the author's opinion of this attitude? (See p. 61)
6. Why is it particularly important for children of immigrants to be instructed in the way the government, institutions and the law work? (See p. 63)
7. How do non-whites react against unemployment? (See p. 64)
8. Composition. (See p. 65)
9. Translate. (See p. 66)

1. Explain in your own words:
   a) Line 12   ...they are poor educational achievers...
   b) Line 14   These facts ... with (similarly) wide currency...
   c) Line 43   ...the demand for under-fives nursery provision should be fully met, ...
1. a) This expression denotes pupils whose results at school are below average. They acquire less skills or abilities than other pupils do.

Note: The expression "poorer educational achievers" can be classified as a **euphemism**. This term means a figure of speech which is used instead of a blunt (grob, derb) or direct expression for something thought to be unpleasant or taboo.
Euphemisms are often used when speaking of death, the human body, lack of intelligence, poverty, etc.

Examples:

	Euphemism	Real meaning
Death:	He was laid to rest.	He was buried.
	He passed away.	He died.
Body:	Where can I wash my hands, please?	Where is the toilet, please?
Unintelligence:	Less able pupils.	Dull, stupid pupils.
	He's a bit strange.	He's crazy.

52

| Poverty: | He is financially embarrassed. | He has debts. |
| | The underprivileged. | The poor. |

Expressing ideas: a) intelligence

He has got a lot of brains.	viel Verstand
His talk is full of wit.	Schlagfertigkeit, geistreich
He had a brainwave.	Geistesblitz, genialer Einfall
He is a brilliant speaker/ scientist/analyst, etc.	scharfsinnig, brillant
He is an able/capable person-	fähig
She is good **at** mathematics, etc.	gut **in** Mathematik, usw.
He is quick **at** learning.	Er lernt schnell.
The ability **to do** something; to be able **to do** something.	(with infinitive)
The capability **of doing** sth; to be capable **of doing** sth.	(with – ing form)
An **intelligent** child/person, etc.	natürliche, angeborene Intelligenz
An intellectual writer/ scientist, etc.	Jemand, der sich Wissen erarbeitet hat; durch geistige Arbeit erworben hat.

---

b) lack of intelligence

It is	silly (dumm) foolish (närrisch) unwise (unklug) imbecilic (verrückt)	to think/say/react, etc....
It would be	imbecility idiocy	to ... Es wäre eine Dummheit/ Verrücktheit zu ...
This	act/behaviour, etc. is an example of great stupidity/ foolishness, etc.	... ein Beispiel für große Dummheit/Verrückt- heit, usw.

Word field: a) intelligence

brightness	Klugheit	brilliant	hochbegabt
prudence	Klugheit, Umsicht	gifted	begabt
brain(s)		capable ⎫	fähig
wit(s)	Verstand, Gehirn	able ⎭	
sense			
cleverness	Schlauheit, Durch-	clever	klug, schlau,
cunning	triebenheit	cunning	durchtrieben
		highbrow	intellektuell,
			anspruchsvoll

b) lack of intelligence

imbecility ⎫		dull	dumm, langsam,
foolishness ⎬	Dummheit	feeble-	dümmlich
stupidity ⎭		minded	
incapacity	Unfähigkeit	ignorant	unwissend
incompetence	Unvermögen	lowbrow	anspruchslos
		backward	zurückgeblieben
		moronic	idiotisch

1. b) this expression means that the facts are accepted by a large number of people.
   or:... are considered to be true by the majority of people.
   or: A lot of people have the same opinion.

      Currency: 1. (Geld-)Währung
                            2. vorherrschende/geltende Meinung, weit verbreite-
   te Annahme

1. c) Parents desire a place where their children, who are under five years old, are taken care of while the parents are at work. This desire ought to be fulfilled by the state.

Word field: to provide

to supply with	versorgen mit	supplies	Vorräte
to furnish with	ausrüsten,	supply	Versorgung,
to equip with	ausstatten mit	provision	Bereit-
			stellung
		equipment	Ausrüstung
to deliver	liefern	delivery	Lieferung

2. Analyse the stylistic device which the author uses in the second sentence of his article.

The author employs three words with the same vowel sound, preceded and followed by different consonants: "Pubs, clubs, buses". This is a rhetorica device called "assonance". At the same time there is the sound "b" in each word. The author wants to catch the reader's attention, he uses these three words with the purpose of impressing upon the reader the fact that race relations are indeed frequently discussed among the British.

Notes:
1. Stylistic (or: rhetorical) devices are an intentional change from what is "normal" in everyday English so as to persuade the reader/listener effectively.
2. Assonance:
   This is a stylistic device using words containing identical vowel sounds.
   (Advertising makes frequent use of assonances, e.g. for a restaurant: "Wine and dine from nine to twelve".
   Or: "Over to Dover", for a Channel Ferry boat.)
3. Alliteration:
   Words with identical consonants at the beginning, e. g. "From top to toe" (Vom Scheitel bis zur Sohle), or: "Round the rocks runs a river".

Expressing ideas: the use of language

The author				
	makes use of			the stylistic device of...
	uses	verwendet		
	employs			
				assonance
	resorts to	greift zurück auf		a vogue word
	selects	wählt ... aus		

These words, expressions, terms, etc.				
	denote	bezeichnen		the concept of ...
	express	drücken aus		
	signify	bedeuten		
	mean	bedeuten		the idea of ...
	imply	deuten an		
	hint at	deuten an		etc.
	allude to	spielen an auf		
	emphasize	betonen		
	convey	vermitteln		
	conjure up	beschwören (herauf)		
	define	legen fest		

The author uses this word		
	in the literal sense.	(im wörtlichen Sinn)
	in a figurative sense.	(im übertragenen Sinn)

The usage of this term, expression, etc.	is		
		literary	literarisch
		formal	formell, förmlich
		informal	informell, zwanglos
		familiar	alltäglich, gewöhnlich
		colloquial	umgangssprachlich
		slang	nachlässiger Jargon gewisser Gruppen/Schichten
		common	geläufig, verbreitet
		current	geläufig, verbreitet

Word field: elements of language

sound	Laut	term	Begriff, Bezeichnung
letter	Buchstabe	expression	Wendung
syllable	Silbe	phrase	Wendung
stylistic device	Stilmittel		
idiom	idiomatische Wendung		
	(It rained cats and dogs.)		
wording (of a text)	Formulierung, Wortlaut	key word	Kennwort, Losung
		catch word	Schlagwort
word order	Wortstellung	vogue word	Modewort

3. Explain the expression "racial melting pot" (line 5 – 6).

In the literal sense, a melting pot is a big container in which metals can be made liquid by heating. In their liquid form different metals can mix and form a new metal, an alloy. Copper and zinc, for example, combine together to make brass.

In this context "racial melting pot" is used in a figurative sense: It denotes a place where people live who belong to the white, black and brown races, i. e. the British, the Afro-Caribbeans and the Asians. The author uses this expression metaphorically.

Alloy = Legierung; copper = Kupfer; brass = Messing;

Notes:
1. Metaphor ['metəfə]
A metaphor is a phrase which describes one thing by stating another thing which it can be compared with.

Examples:

Metaphor	**Meaning**
The old man's snowy hair.	The old man's white hair.
He has a heart of stone.	He is hard and merciless.
"Come here", he thundered.	"Come here", he shouted loudly.

2. Simile [ˈsiməli]

A simili makes a comparison between two things, as does a metaphor, but uses the words "as" or "like".

Examples:
His hair was **as** white **as** snow.
Or: ... **like** a lion's mane.
The two brothers are **as like as** two peas. (Erbsen)

3. Imagery

Imagery is the collective term for metaphors and similes. Imagery is used to make texts more vivid and thus leave a lasting impression on the reader.
The use of imagery is also meant to lead to a better understanding of the essential ideas in a text.

collective term = Oberbegriff; essential = wesentlich

4. a) Which arguments are commonly put forward to account for race problems in Britain?

   b) Analyse the way in which the author counters these arguments.

a) In the text there are three explanations for race problems. In the first place the number of immigrants is considered to be too high. Secondly, the opinion prevails that it was only people not trained for a job in their mother countries who immigrated. Lastly, immigrants are not thought to be as well qualified as whites because they have less success at schools and universities.

b) The author does not resort to wordy explanations in opposing these arguments. In line 14 he concisely states: "These facts ... are all wrong". He bases his counter-arguments on facts and figures. He indicates the exact proportion of coloured immigrants to whites. In the same way he compares the unemployment rates of whites, Asians and West Indians with O-levels. Finally, he gives a brief account of how West Indians were induced to immigrate after the war, and what qualifications they had acquired before leaving their home for Britain.

| to counter | widerlegen | wordy | wortreich, weitschweifig |
| to give an account of | berichten | concise | kurz und bündig, knapp |

58

| the proportion of … to… | das (Zahlen)Verhältnis zwischen … und … |
| to acquire a qualification | eine Fähigkeit erwerben |

Note: The passage from line 14 to line 24 may be called an argumentation (or: argumentative type of text).

In this argumentation the author first presents the commonly accepted facts. He goes on by giving a **subjective** evaluation: "… are all wrong". In support of this statement he presents his own findings.

In the main, an argumentative text is aimed at convincing the reader of the author's view.

Word family: compounds with "counter"

to counteract	vereiteln, entgegenwirken	This rebellion will counteract the government's decision.
to counterbalance to counterpoise to countervail	die Waage halten, aufwiegen, ausgleichen	What can be done to counterbalance the military superiority of the USA/CIS?
a countermeasure (against)	Gegenmaßnahme	The Asians are demanding that the government takes countermeasures.
the counterpart of (a person or thing)	Gegenstück	The German "Bürgermeister" is the counterpart of the English "mayor".
a counterweight to	Gegengewicht	The race laws are not an effective counterweight to discrimination.

Expressing ideas: general acceptance

This	argument belief opinion view impression idea concept thought	is	widely usually generally commonly currently	accepted by ...

Word field: qualities of arguments

a strong	gut, stark	
a weighty	gewichtig	argument
a convincing	überzeugend	

a consistent	logisch, folgerichtig	
a weak	schwach	
a feeble	schwach	argument
an inconsistent	widersprüchlich	

an argument that fails to convince – ein Argument, das nicht überzeugt

5. According to the text, the British and the French share the unwillingness to accept different races. What ist the author's opinion of this attitude?

The author puts forward the argument that the British and the French have had close contacts again and again with different races. Both nations have thus gained an insight into the customs, beliefs and mentalities of non-whites from Africa, Asia and the Caribbean. By saying: "... in spite of ... the white British like the French remain defensive", (line 29) he indirectly expresses his belief that they should be better prepared to find a solution to racial problems.

Expressing ideas. a) segregation, discrimination

to segregate	absondern, trennen, isolieren
to set apart	
to discriminate against someone	jemand benachteiligen, diskriminieren
to treat someone worse than others	jemand schlechter behandeln als andere
to discriminate in favour of ...	zugunsten von ... benachteiligen
to deny someone equal rights	jemand die gleichen Rechte verwehren
to force into a ghetto	in ein Ghetto zwängen
racial segregation	Rassentrennung
segregated schools for racial groups	getrennte Schulen für ...
the segregation of an ethnic group	die Isolierung einer ethnischen Gruppe

b) integration

The	integration assimilation absorption	Aufnahme, Integration, das Aufnehmen	of different races in ...

to allow to	join in mix with unite with become part of		the white society

to grant equal rights to	die gleichen Rechte zugestehen
to accept as full citizens	als gleichberechtigte Mitbürger akzeptieren
to live/work side by side	zusammen, miteinander...

6. Why is it particularly important for children of immigrants to be instructed in the way the government, institutions and the law work? (line 46)

The parents of these children emigrated mainly to earn a living in the host country. The political, social and legal background of their native countries often differ considerably. In most cases, these parents will not be able to explain to their children the principles, rules and rights affecting every member of society.

Moreover, immigrants tend to keep to themselves. This behaviour often leads to the formation of ghetto-like districts, which deprive their children of the chance of experiencing both, what privileges they are entitled to and what laws they are subject to in society at large.

host country	Gastland
to affect	hier: berühren, angehen
to deprive someone of	die Möglichkeit nehmen (berauben)
to be entitled to	ein Anrecht haben auf
to be subject to	unterworfen sein, unterstehen

Expressing ideas: a) right – rights

Immigrants	have a right to … have a just claim to have a legal/lawful/ legitimate claim to …	haben ein Recht auf … haben einen gerechten/ rechtmäßigen Anspruch auf haben einen gesetzlichen Anspruch auf

b) duty – duties

It is our	duty obligation responsibility commitment task	Pflicht Verpflichtung Verantwortung Verpflichtung Aufgabe	to help them. to support… etc.
It is up to us to …		Es liegt an uns …	
We are	due to… expected to …	Es wird von uns erwartet, daß …	
We are	bound to obliged to	verpflichtet	accept them, etc.

Word field: great importance

Something is of	prime	allererster	
	major	größerer	
	decisive	entscheidender	importance.
	crucial	entscheidender	
	vital	lebenswichtiger	

Something is essential for ...   wesentlich, wichtig, unentbehrlich für ...

the	significance	Bedeutung	of this problem
	urgency	Dringlichkeit	of this development
	gravity	Ernst	of this situation
	seriousness	Ernst	etc.

the heart of the matter	die Hauptsache, das Wesent-
the (most) essential part of	liche, das Wichtigste

the	core	of something	der Kern einer Sache
	gist		das Wichtigste

The core of discrimination is fear and prejudice.
What is the gist of this report?

7. How do non-whites react against unemployment?

Home Office research reveals that non-whites have accustomed themselves
to accepting any job available, even if they do not like it.
Similarly, they do not shy away from doing work beneath their abilities,
which, of course, means earning a smaller income. In contrast with many
whites, they are ready to reduce their ambitions rather than be on the dole.

Home Office	Innenministerium
to shy away from	zurückschrecken vor
to be on the dole	Arbeitslosengeld erhalten

63

Expressing ideas: reaction

Study the prepositions:

1. to react **against**

to take action against something unpleasant, harmful, dangerous, etc.

They react against unemployment by accepting any job.

Sie reagieren auf ..., indem sie ...

2. to react **to**

to behave differently as a result

She reacted immediately to the news of her win.

Sie reagierte/antwortete sofort auf...

3. to react **with**

technical term: oxygen reacts with quicksilver

Their	answer to			
	response to	Antwort auf	this threat is ...
	reply to			

or:

In answer to
In response to   this danger, they ... **Als** Antwort **auf**
In reply to

Study the structures:

The immigrants answer unemployment **with** the acception of any job.
Or: The immigrants answer unemployment **by** accep**ting** any job.

8. Composition

In the last paragraph of his article, the author makes some suggestions about how to ameliorate race relations. Do you think they are sufficient to integrate the non-whites? State your reasons.

In my view, it is not enough to improve the material well-being of non-whites by providing them with better housing, schools and jobs. The heart of the matter is prejudice – it is of prime importance to do away with this.

Secondly, it is essential to give non-whites responsibilities (not just for the litter in the streets) and functions in the framework of society; as members of parents' associations of kindergartens and schools on one level, or in positions of authority within key social institutions (such as the courts, army or police force) on another.

A third point is the encouragement of tolerance on the part of whites for the non-whites' cultural heritage, religious beliefs, moral code and folkore.

Moreover, such tolerance could be fostered by more personal contacts between the different racial groups; these contacts might take the form of invitations to one another's homes, the cooperation in the solution of common problems or in whites helping non-whites to cope with the complexities of social institutions.

If all of the above-mentioned initiatives are taken, there is bound to be more mutual understanding and a resulting amelioration in the racial situation in Britain.

| to foster | fördern | mutual | gegenseitig |

9. Translate

Attitudes Towards the Police

Non-whites, particularly West Indians, are much more hostile than whites to the police.

The reasons for this are complex. For a long period there was evidence of racism among police officers and non-whites were subjected to some racial abuse and harassment by police, especially when the controversial stop-and-search law was used on the streets.

However, the police force has been the only institution to take the 1981 riots seriously and significant changes have occurred. The new breed of police chiefs, sensitive to social problems, has insisted on race relations training for their men and community policing has made great strides in improving the general climate on the streets. All cadets at Henley Police College undergo race relations training and spend some time in inner city areas with high ethnic minority concentrations before starting work.

But Home Office Ministers admit more needs to be done and, in particular, there are still far too few non-white policemen on the streets. As the recent riots have shown, a misunderstanding, a rumour or a blunder is enough to undo years of community policing work.

Vocabulary

hostile	showing dislike; unfriendly	feindselig
evidence **of**	proof **of**	Beweis **für**
subject to	caused to experience	ausgesetzt, unterworfen
abuse	wrong, bad use	Mißbrauch, Mißachtung
harassment		Belästigung
to harass	to worry, annoy or pester someone	belästigen
controversial	causing much disagreement	umstritten
breed	here: kind or class of people	Generation, Rasse (Zucht)
to police	to control; to keep a watch on	überwachen
to make great strides in	here: to make good progress	große Fort-schritte er-zielen
to undergo (training)	here: to be taught/ instructed	geschult werden
blunder	very stupid mistake	grober Fehler, Schnitzer

Das Verhältnis zur Polizei

Farbige, insbesondere von den Westindischen Inseln, stehen der Polizei sehr viel feindseliger gegenüber als Weiße.

Die Gründe dafür sind vielschichtig. Lange Zeit hindurch war Rassismus unter Polizeibeamten unverkennbar, und Farbige waren wegen ihrer Rasse Übergriffen und Belästigungen ausgesetzt, besonders als das umstrittene Gesetz über Festnahme und Durchsuchung von Straßenpassanten angewandt wurde.

Dennoch war die Polizei die einzige Institution, die die Unruhen von 1981 ernst nahm, und seither sind wichtige Veränderungen eingetreten. Die neue Generation von leitenden Polizeibeamten, die ein Gespür für soziale Probleme hat, bestand darauf, daß ihre Männer im Umgang mit Menschen anderer Rassen ausgebildet wurden, und die bürgernahe Ausübung der polizeilichen Aufgaben hat große Fortschritte erzielt in der Klimaverbesserung auf den Straßen. Alle Polizeischüler am Henley Police College werden im Umgang mit Menschen anderer Rassen ausgebildet und müssen eine gewisse Ausbildungszeit in innerstädtischen Bezirken ableisten, in denen sich starke ethnische Minderheiten zusammendrängen, ehe sie ihre Diensttätigkeit antreten.

Aber im britischen Innenministerium wird zugegeben, daß noch mehr getan werden muß, und daß es insbesondere noch viel zu wenig farbige Polizisten in den Straßen gibt. Die jüngsten Unruhen haben gezeigt, daß ein Mißverständnis, ein Gerücht oder ein grober Fehler genügen, um jahrelange bürgernahe Polizeiarbeit zunichte zu machen.

Polish up your grammar

Negative prefixes

Preliminary remark:

The use of hyphens between the negative prefix and the base is problematical, dictionaries contradict each other. The hyphens in the following list are according to "Collins, German-English Dictionary", (See also note at the end of this chapter).

1. Non

Non ist mainly added to adjectives and nouns giving the meaning "not" .

a) Adjectives

non-committal	not expressing a clear opinion, promise, intention, etc.	zurückhaltend, unverbindlich
	not existing,	nicht existieren
non existent	not existent	nicht vorhanden sein
nondescript	ordinary-looking, without interesting qualities	unauffällig, schwer beschreibbar
nonpareil (lit.)	so excellent as to have no equal	unvergleichlich, einzigartig
non-resident	not living in a certain place	nicht ansässig
non-stop	without stopping (travel, flight)	durchgehend, ohne Zwischenaufenthalt, -landung
non-U	not of the upper class (words, behaviour, etc.)	nicht der Oberschicht angehörend
non-violent	not using violence (esp. for political purposes)	gewaltlos

b) Nouns

non-aggression	not attacking non-aggression pact	Nichtangriffs-(pakt)
nonconformist	1. person not thinking, behaving, etc. as most people do	ein unangepaßter Mensch
	2. religious group which has separated from the Church of England	Nonkonformist
nonentity	person of no importance	ein Nichts, eine unbedeutende Figur

non-fiction	literature other than poetry, plays, stories and novels	Sachbücher, -literatur
non-proliferation	keeping atomic weapons in only the same amounts and the same countries as at present	die Nichterhö- hung der Zahl/ die Nichtweiter- gabe von Atom- waffen
nonsense	1. something with no meaning or against common sense	Unsinn, dummes Zeug
	2. humorous poetry, often meaningless	Nonsensverse
non-intervention	taking no part in affairs of other countries, governments, etc.	Nichteinmischung

2. Un

Un is added to adjectives, participles meaning: "the opposite of".
a) Adjectives: unfair, unwise, unbelievable, unimpeachable (tadellos)
b) Participles: unexpected, unrivalled, unseeing (blind) unflinching (furchtlos).

3. In, il, im, ir

They function in the same way as "un".
a) inescapable, inexact, etc.   These prefixes are
b) illogical, illegitimate, etc.   mainly found in learned
c) impolite, immovable, etc.   words of Latin or French
d) irresponsible, irrelevant, etc.   origin.

4. Dis (in the same way as "un")

to dislike, to disobey, to disband (a club – auflösen)
discontent, disadvantageous
discontinuation – Einstellung, Abbruch
disembarkation – Ausschiffung, von Bord gehen

Note: The hyphen

There are only rules of thumb (Daumenregeln) for the use of hyphens between a prefix and the base. GCE* discerns the following trends:

1. A hyphen is used in cases where the second part has a capital letter: un-English, un-American, non-U;
2. in words where the lack of a hyphen may suggest wrong pronounciation as in pre-eminent, to co-operate, to re-establish, etc.;
3. American writers tend to use fewer hyphens than British writers do.

* A Grammar of Contemporary English, Longman, 1972, pp 1018; 1066-1067)

4. Tourist Hordes in London

It's that time of the year again, the frantic period between the summer solstice and the autumnal equinox during which Europe finds itself hosting a vast game of musical chairs, played by several million nomads known as tourists. Everywhere you look, from Piccadilly Cir-
5 cus to the Piazza di Spagna, you see them gathered in confused clumps, rubbing their feet and reloading their cameras. There are Germans in Spain, Japanese in Paris and Americans everywhere. It was like this last summer, but not quite as bad. It will be like this next summer − but probably a bit worse. The thing to remember about tourists is that
10 everything that is said about them is true. En masse, they are seen as bovine herds or barbarian hordes; often both.

You would think this would be a great time to be a tourist in London. After all, with the pound still quite weak, a visitor with foreign curren-cy to spend should be able to live in style, make the scene, indulge his
15 fondest fantasies, right? You could start off, say, by going to Savile Row to have a suit made by the celebrated street's most celebrated tailor, Huntsman. Then nip over to Jermyn Street to order a dozen candy-striped shirts from Turnbull & Asser. Later on, dinner at Le Gavroche (arguably, the finest French restaurant in town), and finally
20 to the theater to take in London's hottest musical, "Starlight Express".

Not to put too fine a point on it, London this summer has been overrun by a horde of foreigners the likes of which hasn't been seen since the Roman legions pulled up stakes and went home 1.600 years ago. One
25 is tempted to compare the crowds that jam Piccadilly at lunchtime these days to the massed and twisted bodies that fill Michelangelo's great vision of the damned on the end wall of the Sistine Chapel. But, then, none of Michelangelo's condemned are wearing backpacks. In all, nearly 9 million foreign visitors are expected to stream through the
30 greater London area this year. And while shopkeepers are understand-ably delighted by the resulting influx of dollars, lire, marks, dinars and francs, less fortunate locals are starting to understand what the Australian aborigines must have felt like when the white men began pouring into Botany Bay.

35 It's not only the theatergoers and gourmets who have been affected by
the invasion of foreigners. Humble commuters, too, are feeling the
tourist heel on their necks. Catching a tube, train or doubledecker bus
has become almost impossible, so clogged are they with gigantic
Australian, American and Scandinavian teenagers bowed under back-
40 packs and bedrolls the size of telephone booths. Entrances to the
underground are particularly difficult to negotiate, it apparently being
the custom of these visitors to wait until they reach the portals before
stopping to unfold large maps of the city to find out where they are.

For resident Londoners quite understandably driven to seek peace and
45 quiet and spiritual nourishment away from the seething mass, it is no
comfort to step into the vaulted cool of Westminster Abbey − not
when one is likely to be trampled at any minute by 50 Germans seeking
the tombs of Henry VII and Elizabeth I. Nor is there any refuge to be
found these days in the normally silent National Gallery. Try to con-
50 centrate your thoughts on a favourite masterpiece − say the "Wilton
Triptych", painted in about 1395 when the only tourists were Flemish
weavers − and your reverie will invariably be shattered by a loud,
female American voice shrieking, "Look, George, the Wilton Triptych. It's very old".

55 No relief in sight: Shoved, pushed, starved, deprived of decent bespoke
clothing − the average Londoner cannot even console himself with the
knowledge that soon the invaders will have gone. The figures show
they now stay longer, and that every year there are more of them. In
1974 a mere 8.5 million visitors came to the whole of Britain. By 1984
60 the number had climbed to almost 14 million; this year will bring a
million more than that.

In a parliamentary debate on tourism late last year, a less than en-
thusiastic Tory M.P. quoted the text of a new prayer promulgated by
the Orthodox Church in Greece asking the Lord to have mercy on
65 Greek cities and islands "which are scourged by the world touristic
wave" and asking protection "from these contemporary Western invaders". But alas, the M.P. was a voice in the wilderness, drowned out
by a chorus of reminders that tourism now earns Britain more foreign
currency − an estimated $6.5 billion this year alone − than any other
70 industry except oil.

72

Given the importance of tourism to Britain's ailing economy, it's hardly surprising that *Sunday Times* columnist John Huxley took it upon himself last month to publicly scold what he described as the country's "surly taxi drivers, sloppy hotel and restaurant staff, dozy tourism of-
75 ficials . . .''. But perhaps these folk should be considered the noble defenders of Britain's insular attitudes, deserving of praise from a grateful nation. For it may be that only traditional bloody-mindedness, loathing of things and people foreign, and good old British idleness will preserve some remnant of a once-great nation's character.

I. Vocabulary

frantic	marked by hurried and disordered activity	rasend, toll, (wahnsinnig)
summer solstice	(June, 22th)	Sommersonnenwende
autumnal equinox	(September, 22th)	Tag- und Nacht-gleiche im Herbst
to host	to act as a host at (a party, a meeting, etc.)	Gastgeber sein
a game of musical chairs	a game in which, when the music stops, each person tries to find a chair to sit on, although there is one chair too few	(ein Tanzspiel) "Reise nach Jerusalem"
a clump	here: a mass of	Haufen, Klumpen, Gruppe
bovine herd	like a cow or an ox	Rinder(-herde)
indefatigable	that shows no sign of tiring	unermüdlich
rube (US.slang)	an unsophisticated farmer	Bauerntölpel

vulgarian	person whose behaviour is considered unsuitable and vulgar	ungesitteter, pöbelhafter Mensch
patron	here: regular customer	Stammkunde
to cultivate	here: to give careful attention to	umhegen, umsorgen
in style	in a grand way	stilvoll, vornehm
to make the scene	to make a big impact	groß herauskommen
to indulge something	here: to let oneself have one's wish	einem Wunsch nachgeben
to nip (over to)	here: to hurry	eilen, einen Sprung hinübermachen zu
arguably	here: able to be supported with reasons, though not proven; probably	sehr wahrscheinlich, wohl
not to put too fine a point on it	if I may speak the plain (unpleasant) truth	geradeheraus/ohne Umschweife sagen
to pull up stakes (esp. AmE)	to give up	alles aufgeben
to jam	to crowd with people so that movement is difficult or impossible	verstopfen, versperren
backpack	rucksack, knapsack	Rucksack
a local	here: a person who lives in the place he is in	Ortsansässiger, Einheimischer
an aborigine (aboriginal)	member of a group, tribe, etc. that has lived in a place from the earliest times, esp. in Australia	Ureinwohner

74

gourmet	a person who knows a lot about food and drink and is good at choosing what should be combined together	Feinschmecker
commuter	a person who makes a regular journey of some distance between work and home	Pendler
heel	back part of the foot or shoe	Ferse; Schuhabsatz
to clog	here: (to cause) to become blocked	verstopfen, hemmen
to be bowed [baud] under	bent down under	gebeugt unter
to negotiate	here: to go (safely) through	(ein Hindernis) über-winden, passieren
to seethe	to move about as if boiling	brodeln, sieden
tomb [tu:m]	large grave	Grab(-stätte)
refuge (for)	place that provides protection or shelter (from a danger)	Zufluchtsort
reverie	pleasant thoughts and dreams while awake	Träumerei
to shriek	to cry out with a high sound	kreischen
to shove	to push, esp. in a rough and careless way	(beiseite) schieben, drängen
to deprive of	to take away from, to prevent from using	jemandem etwas ent-ziehen, vorenthalten

decent	socially acceptable, not causing shame or shock to others	anständig, ordentlich
bespoke (BE) (of clothes)	specially made to one's measurements	maßgeschneidert
to console oneself (with)	to give comfort or sympathy to oneself in times of disappointment or sadness	(sich) trösten mit
to promulgate	to spread (a belief, an idea, etc.) widely among large numbers of people	verkünden, verbreiten, bekannt machen
to scourge	to cause great harm or suffering to; to beat with a whip	züchtigen, quälen; geißeln
ailing	to be ill and grow weak	kränklich, leidend, darniederliegend
surly	(seeming) angry, bad-mannered	mürrisch, schroff, verdrießlich
sloppy	not careful or thorough enough	nachlässig, schlampig
dozy	sleepy	schläfrig, träge
bloody-mindedness	having the desire to oppose the wishes of others, often unreasonably	Sturheit, Widerwilligkeit, Widersetzlichkeit
loathing of	a feeling of disgust for	Abscheu, Abneigung, (Ekel)
remnant	a part that remains	Überrest, Überbleibsel

Pitfalls in the language

1. line 14: to indulge something — etwas nachgeben
             to indulge a person — jemandem nachgeben
             to indulge **in** sth. — sich einer Sache hingeben, einer Leidenschaft frönen, sich etwas gönnen

2. line 32: **a** local — Einheimischer, Ortsansässiger
             the local — Stammlokal, -kneipe

3. line 35: a gourmet ['guəmei] — Feinschmecker
             a gourmand ['guəmənd] — gefräßiger Mensch, Vielfraß

4. line 55: decent — ordentlich, anständig, vernünftig
             German "dezent" (= zurückhaltend, unauffällig, unaufdringlich) is in English: "discreet, unobtrusive".

5. line 67: to drown out — übertönen, überschreien
             to drown — 1. ertrinken
                        2. ertränken

II. Questions on the text.

1. What picture of Europe does the author present in the first paragraph? (See p. 74)

2. In the first paragraph the author uses **alliteration** (Lines 4 – 5). Analyse form and meaning of this stylistic device. (See p. 75)

3. What typical behaviour of tourists does the author point to when he uses the words "clumps" (l. 5), "herds" (l. 11) and "hordes" (l. 11)? (See p. 75)

4. In the second paragraph, the author gives two reasons why a holiday in London should be a success for foreigners. Find these reasons and analyse the way in which the author presents them. (See p. 78)

5. Which **associations** does the author arouse by citing two historic events? (3rd paragraph, lines 24 and 33) (See p. 79)

6. Describe the tone of the text in the fourth paragraph (line 35 to 43). By what means does the author produce this tone? (See p. 81)

7. There are many stereotyped jokes about Americans who go sightseeing in Europe. Explain the one in lines 53 – 54. (See p. 83)

8. Describe the features of the British temperament which – in the author's view – can best cope with the tourist onslaught in summer. (See p. 84)

9. Summarize the first paragraph. (See p. 86)

10. Composition.
    The text of the prayer of the Orthodox Church in Greece says: ". . . cities and islands which are scourged by the world touristic wave" (line 65). What reasons are there for denoting tourism a "scourge" in countries attracting a lot of holidaymakers? (See p. 86)

11. Translate. (See p. 87)

1. What picture of Europe does the author present in the first paragraph?

The author portrays Europe in summer overwhelmed by a record-breaking number of tourists. From north to south the Continent is jammed with people from all parts of the world.

the **C**ontinent — Europe without the British Isles
a   **c**ontinent — Africa, Europe, Asia, etc.

Expressing ideas: to invade in large numbers — überfallen

(compounds with "over-")

Tourists, visitors, etc.	overrun overflow overcrowd overwhelm	a place.	— überrennen, herfallen über — überschwemmen — überfüllen (-völkern) — überwältigen

2. In the first paragraph the author uses **alliteration** (lines 4 – 5). Analyse form and meaning of this stylistic device.

In lines 4 – 5 the author employs the expression ". . . from Piccadilly Circus to the Piazza of Spagna". These two place-names begin with the same consonant sounds [p] and [s]. The author employs this stylistic device to help stress his claim that tourists are ubiquitous, no matter where you are in Europe.

ubiquitous — formal English for "everywhere" (— allgegenwärtig)

3. What typical behaviour of tourists does the author point to when he uses the words "clumps" (line 5), "herds", (line 11) and "hordes" (line 11)?

In the author's description, tourists never appear individually or even in small groups of two or three. They seem to be in the habit of crowding together, just as some kinds of animals cling together, driven by a deep-rooted herd instinct. This behaviour reveals a lack of individuality.

Pitfalls in the language: individual

a) individually (adv.)   — 1. einzeln, jeder für sich
                              2. betont eigenwillig

79

b) individuality	— Eigenart, bestimmte Art, Einzelgängertum, Individualität
individualism	— Vorstellung von den besonderen Rechten und Freiheiten des einzelnen (in der Gesellschaft); Individualismus
c) individual (adj.)	— 1. einzeln each individual tree — jeder einzelne Baum
	2. zugeschnitten auf, besonders geeignet für; individual service for handicapped people — eine Hilfe, besonders für Behinderte
	3. persönlich, von ausgeprägter Eigenart his individual style — sein persönlicher Stil
d) an individual (n.)	— 1. ein einzelner
	2. (verächtlich:) Person, Individuum

I wouldn't trust that individual. — Ich würde dieser Person nicht trauen.

Expressing ideas: to be in the habit of — gewohnt sein

Someone is used to do**ing** sth. — *gewohnt sein, etw. zu tun*

Tourists are not used to explor**ing** the town individually.

It is	usual	for	people,			— *Gewöhnlich,*
	customary	for	tourists,		to do something.	*üblicherweise . . .*
	normal	for	etc.			

to do something	out of habit	— *etwas gewohnheitsmäßig tun*
	by habit	

the force of habit — *die Macht der Gewohnheit*
Man is a creature of habit. — *Der Mensch ist ein Gewohnheitstier.*

It is a | custom | to do sth. — *Es ist eine (An-)Gewohnheit,*
| habit | | *Sitte . . .*

In England | you get used to | drinking tea | *In England*
| you accustom yourself to | at any time | *gewöhnt man*
| | of the day. | *sich daran . . .*

I'm not in the habit of | getting | *Ich bin*
I'm not accustomed to | up early. | *nicht daran*
I'm not used to | | *gewöhnt . . .*

Gerund: He is used to do**ing** sth. — *Er ist gewöhnt, etwas zu tun.*

Infinitive: He used to **do** sth. — *Früher tat usw. er etwas*
(Habits that existed in *oft . . .*
the past.) *Früher pflegte er . . .*

We | used to | go for long walks. — *Früher machten wir oft*
| would | | *lange Spaziergänge.*

Harmful habits: He became addicted to drugs. — *Er wurde drogenab-*
hängig.

an addict — *ein (Drogen-)Abhängiger*
an alcoholic — *ein Alkoholiker*

81

4. In the second paragraph, the author gives two reasons why a holiday in London should be a success for foreigners. Find these reasons and analyse the way in which the author presents them.

The first reason can be found in the phrase ". . . with the pound still quite weak, . . .". Foreigners, provided with a strong currency, find that things are cheaper in London. This enables them to make purchases and to enjoy pleasures which they cannot afford at home. The author states this reason in an "explicit way", using clear and direct words.

The second reason is the fact that the Metropolis offers a wide range of high-standard attractions, such as distinguished shops, exquisite food or great theatrical performances. The reader is given these facts to consider and can draw his own conclusions as to whether a trip to London will make for a successful holiday, without the author's expressing his opinion in a direct way.

This type of presentation of ideas may be described as "implicit".

Note on authors' presenting a fact, an idea, an argument, etc.:

an explicit representation of	– eine deutliche, klare, direkte Darstellung
an implicit representation of	– eine indirekte, umschreibende Darstellung (bei der der Leser seine eigenen Schlüsse ziehen kann).

explicit – to represent something in clear words
implicit – not to represent something plainly; to leave it to the reader to reach his own conclusions on . . .

82

Word field: holiday — Ferien, Urlaub

BE holiday/holidays	— *Ferien, Urlaub*
AmE vacation	— *Ferien, Urlaub*
BE vacation	— *Semesterferien (an der Universität)*
recreation	— *Erholung*
a holidaymaker	— *ein Urlauber*
to holiday	— *Ferien/Urlaub machen* We were holidaying in Scotland.
to go somewhere for one's holiday	— *in den Ferien irgendwo hinfahren* Where are you going for your holiday?
a holiday a day off	— *ein freier Tag*

5. Which associations does the author arouse by citing two historic events? (3rd paragraph, lines 24 and 33).

Both historic events remind us of countries being conquered and their populations subjugated by foreign invaders. The author establishes a link in the readers' imagination between these conquests and the influx of tourists into London with these two examples.

Note on stylistic devices: **association — Assoziation, gedankliche Verknüpfung**

This term is used for connecting (or: linking) similar ideas/feelings/thoughts, etc. in the readers' mind.

Expressing ideas: a) association — Assoziation

| The | author
text
statement
etc. | conjures up
stirs up
arouses
evokes | } — *beschwört herauf*

} — *ruft hervor* | an association
by . . .
through . . . |

| He | connects
links | this idea
event
situation
fact
etc. | with . . . |

| This | idea
statement
opinion
event, etc. | is associated with . . . (. . . *ist verknüpft mit* . . .) |

b) example — Beispiel

| The author | quotes
cites
gives | } — *führt an* | an example **of**. . .
an instance **of**. . . | } — *ein Bei-*
spiel
für . . . |

| This example | demonstrates
illustrates
clarifies | } — *zeigt*

— *macht deutlich* | the . . .
that (he) . . . |

| I'd like to quote an example | to prove
to support
in support of | my argument(s). |

– *Ich möchte ein Beispiel für meine Behauptung anführen.*

This is a	concrete	– *konkret*	
	appropriate	– *passend*	example of . . .

to serve as **an** example **of** – *als Beispiel dienen für* . . .

The author exemplifies (something) by showing/saying, etc. . . .

– *. . . gibt ein Beispiel für . . ., indem er zeigt/sagt usw. . . .*
– *. . . belegt etwas durch ein Beispiel, indem er . . .*

This exemplification is/is not convincing. – *Diese Belegung/Erläuterung durch Beispiele ist/ist nicht überzeugend.*

exemplary – *beispielhaft, vorbildlich*

6. Describe the tone of the text in the 4th paragraph (line 35 to 43). By what means does the author produce this tone?

Dealing with crammed buses and trains, the author expresses the inconveniences created by tourists in a humorous way. The author causes amusement by exaggerating the facts. His sense of humour reveals itself in the claim that teenagers from America, etc. are "gigantic" (line 38) or that "it is the custom of these visitors . . ." (line 40) to block the station entrances while reading their huge maps.

A comic effect also springs from a hyperbole (i.e. exaggeration); the author says that the teenagers' backpacks and bedrolls are "the size of telephone booths" (line 40).

Expressing ideas: a humorous tone — humorvoll

The text	is full of abounds in	amusing comic absurd ludicrous	remarks exaggerations etc.

The humour	springs from is produced by originates in	understatement exaggeration etc.

The author	aims at intends to produce	a comic effect by	saying . . . comparing . . . etc.

This	comparison hyperbole exaggeration	causes/raises laughter. is intended to amuse the reader. makes the reader laugh silently to himself.

Pitfalls in the language:

1. comic (adj.)
   comical
   - funny, humorous, causing laughter – lustig
   - amusing in a strange/odd way – spaßig, ulkig, komisch, wunderlich

2. humour
   (humorous)
   wit (witty)
   - Humor, Scherz, Spaß (humorvoll)
   - clever **and** amusing at the same time – geistreicher Humor/Witz (witzig)

3. good-humoured
   - 1. gutmütig
     2. gut gelaunt/aufgelegt
     (opposite: bad-tempered)

7. There are many stereotyped jokes about Americans who go sightseeing in Europe. Explain the one in lines 53 – 54.

In Europe, there is a tendency to look down on Americans because of Europe's longer tradition of culture. This attitude is strengthened by the Americans' awe of (1) everything that is old. It also fits into the pattern that Americans are believed to be more practically-minded and less sensitive to the arts. This cliché is exemplified in the lady's comment on the painting: ''It's very old.''

(1) awe of — Ehrfurcht vor

Word field: cliché — Klischeevorstellung

---

cliché	— *Klischee, -vorstellung, Gemeinplatz, abgedroschenes Schlagwort*
stereotype	— *eine ständig gebrauchte Wendung, eine abgedroschene Vorstellung von etwas*
commonplace	— *Gemeinplatz*
truism	— *Binsenwahrheit*
platitude	— *nichtssagende Wendung/Vorstellung/Bemerkung usw.*

Expressing ideas: commonplace — Gemeinplatz

This	word expression idea argument etc.	is worn out. (— *abgedroschen*)

This	argument	is so	clear	that there is no
	idea		well-known	need to mention it.
	etc.		common	

This	word	is in such common use	that it has
	expression	has been used so often	(almost)

> lost its meaning.
> become meaningless.

8. Describe the features of the British temperament which — in the author's view — can best cope with the tourist onslaught in summer.

to cope with	— fertig werden mit etwas, einer Sache/Person gewachsen sein
onslaught	— Angriff, Attacke

There are three specific qualities of the British character which the author considers capable of meeting the challenge of the tourist invasion. The first is that the British strongly dislike doing what others expect them to. Furthermore, it is especially foreigners whom they are not particularly fond of. Lastly, the attitude to work ("sloppy . . .", "dozy . . .", "idleness . . .", lines 74 – 78) might keep tourists away from Britain. According to the author, these inherited traits will probably act as a bulwark against the onrush of the tourist hordes.

Word field: to match — mit etwas fertig werden können

---

to be a match for		
to cope with	a person	— *es mit jemandem/etwas*
to be equal to	something	*aufnehmen können*
to be up to		

Expressing ideas: characteristic − charakteristisch

| This . . . | is | characteristic **of** | the British. |
| | | typical **of** | |

Their	character	is marked by . . .
	temperament	(. . . zeichnet sich aus durch . . .)
	mentality	

It is one of their	characteristics	to be . . .
	traits (Charakterzug)	that they . . .
	features (auffallende	
	Eigenschaft)	

Characteristically, the British . . (do, act, behave, etc.) . . .
Es ist charakteristisch für die Briten, daß sie . . .

The most striking characteristic is . . .
Das auffälligste Charaktermerkmal ist . . .

This behaviour (etc.) is	hereditary	
	innate	} − . . . *angeboren.*
	part of their nature.	

They are a	race		
	breed } − *Rasse*	of people who . . .
	type − *Art*	

What are the British like?

89

9. Summarize the first paragraph.

June 22nd to September 22nd is the height of the tourist season in Europe. Not only masses of Americans and Japanese, but also Europeans themselves overrun the Continent at this time of the year. The tourist onslaught increases from year to year, and it can be said that all the unpleasant clichés of tourists are correct.

10. Composition.

The text of the prayer of the Orthodox Church of Greece says: ". . . cities and islands which are scourged by the world touristic wave" (line 65). What reasons are there for denoting tourism a "scourge" in countries attracting a lot of holidaymakers?

One man's 'recreation' is another man's 'scourge', and the darker sides of mass tourism for the countries hosting these mobs are all too apparent.

In the first place, the arrival of crowds of foreigners in small villages and resorts causes a great amount of discomfort and displeasure to the native inhabitants, especially to those who have to earn their money in hotels and restaurants.

The tourists contribute greatly to noise pollution, litter streets and beaches, and are generally conspicuous because of their loud, unruly behaviour and indulgence in alcohol. Any peace and quiet there may have been is lost and the locals' own retreats for recreation are all occupied by the tourists.

A second, and obvious disadvantage of tourism is the destruction of beautiful, natural scenery through the buildings of often ugly hotels, motorways and airports, all of which only cater for the needs of tourists.

A third effect is to push prices − especially those for food and accomodation − through the ceiling; the main sufferers are the local inhabitants, whose wages do not rise by the corresponding amount.

Tourists often show a lack of cultural awareness and an ignorance of local customs and traditions; to recognize this facet, one only has to think of the number of tourists who try to enter Italian churches in inappropriate clothing, e.g. shorts or bathing costumes, or those who insist on bathing nude in countries where this is considered improper. Where tourists do actually take an interest in traditions and folklore, these often degenerate into another part of the tourist industry, something else which can be traded for cash.

Finally, countries dependent on tourism for foreign exchange often invest huge amounts in hotels and attractions which only make a profit during the all too short 'season'. This money would be of more use to the population were it invested in the development of local industry and agriculture. The profits might not be as attractive, but the prospects of long-term employment for the locals and long-term benefits for the country would be far greater.

11. Translation
   Surfing

The most difficult thing of all is getting to your feet on the board. A wave will pass underneath you and not take you along if you try to ride it without any forward momentum of your own. So, when you see your chosen wave coming, you must paddle furiously to match your speed to it. When you feel it lifting you along, you must leap up from the board. In theory, this involves a sinewy press-up and landing planted firmly in the middle of the board. More often, an undignified scramble is punished by an unceremonious ducking, and a weary paddle back to the beach.

It became apparent that good surfers are more than strong swimmers with a sense of balance. They have an uncanny knack for picking the right wave, a knack, which I suspect cannot be learned. Surfing profits from the current enthusiasm for non-team, non-ball-game sports. As hang-gliding, mountain bikes and skateboarding have proved themselves to be more than just passing fads, so surfing, like them, is beginning to be seen as an enormously popular leisure activity.

Lying on the beach is what we used to think it was all about. But idleness is no longer so firmly wedded to leisure. Action holidays of one sort of another seem to be here to stay. Beach holidays now tend to be windsurfing or sailing or parascending holidays rather than a fat paperback and pints of suntan oil. This change has been good for surfing. As the public has begun to be interested, so television and the sponsorship that goes with it have come hurrying along to see what is in it for them.

Surfing was first seen in Tahiti and described by Captain Cook in his journals of 1777 and 1778 and he insists that what he saw was a pastime not connected with work in any way. But surfing was banned from Tahiti by missionaries brim-full of disapproval in 1821.

The founder of 20th century surfing was Duke Paon Kahanamoku, the great Hawaiian swimmer who won the Olympic hundred metres in freestyle in 1912 and 1920. He travelled the world with his surfboards, long unweildy, heavy things, leaving one behind wherever he thought surfing might implant itself.

Vocabulary

momentum	the force gained by movement	Schwung, Triebkraft, Impuls
sinewy	here: strong	kraftvoll, kräftig, stark
a press-up	—	Liegestütz
a scramble	act of moving or climbing, esp. over a rough surface	(Herum-)Krabbeln, Kriechen
a ducking	the act of pushing under water	Eintauchen, Untertauchen
uncanny	mysterious, not natural or usual	ungeheuer, unheimlich
a knack	a special skill or ability, usually the result of practice	Geschicklichkeit, Gewandtheit, Kniff, Trick
a fad	short-lived but keenly followed interest or practice	Liebhaberei, Steckenpferd, Modetorheit, Schrulle, Laune

parascending	—	Drachen-, Fallschirmfliegen, von einem Motorboot gezogen
sponsor(ship)	business that pays for a show, broadcast, sports event, etc.	Geldgeber (Patenschaft, Gönnerschaft)
brim-full	full to the top, overflowing	bis zum Rand gefüllt
unweildy	awkward to move, especially because too large, too heavy, etc.	unhandlich, sperrig

Surfen

Am allerschwierigsten ist es, auf dem Brett zum Stehen zu kommen. Wenn du versuchst, auf einer Welle zu reiten, ohne daß du selbst einen Schwung nach vorn machst, so wird die Welle unter dir durchlaufen, ohne dich mitzunehmen. Sobald du die Welle, die du ausgesucht hast, herankommen siehst, mußt du deshalb heftig paddeln, um dich ihrer Geschwindigkeit anzugleichen. Wenn du das Gefühl hast, daß sie dich mitträgt, mußt du auf dem Brett einen kleinen Sprung machen. Theoretisch ist damit eine Art kraftvoller Liegestütz und eine sichere Landung auf der Mitte des Brettes gemeint. Es kommt häufig vor, daß du für dein lächerliches Herumkrabbeln bestraft wirst: du fällst ins Wasser und mußt mühselig zum Strand zurückpaddeln.

Man erkannte, daß ein guter Surfer mehr ist als nur ein guter Schwimmer, der leicht das Gleichgewicht halten kann. Er ist unheimlich gewandt beim Aussuchen der richtigen Welle, eine Geschicklichkeit, die man, wie ich vermute, nicht lernen kann. Das Surfen profitiert zur Zeit von der Begeisterung für Sportarten, bei denen man keiner Mannschaft angehören muß, und für die man keinen Ball braucht. In derselben Weise, wie sich das Drachenfliegen, Bergtouren mit dem Fahrrad und Skateboardfahren nicht nur als kurzlebige Modetorheiten erwiesen haben, entdeckt man jetzt allmählich, daß Surfen ebenfalls ein sehr beliebter Freizeitsport ist.

Früher dachten wir, daß es nur darum geht, am Strand zu liegen. Aber Freizeit ist nicht mehr so eng mit Faulenzen verbunden. Der Aktivurlaub hat sich anscheinend eingebürgert. Offensichtlich verbringt man heutzutage seine Ferien am Strand eher mit Surfen, Segeln oder Drachenfliegen – wobei man von einem Motorboot gezogen wird, als mit voluminösen Taschenbüchern und mit Kannen voll Sonnenöl. Diese Veränderung war gut für das Surfen. Als sich die Öffentlichkeit allmählich dafür interessierte, haben sich auch das Fernsehen und private Geldgeber eingeschaltet, um herauszufinden, was dabei für sie herausspringt.

Das Surfen wurde erstmals vor Tahiti beobachtet; Captain Cook beschrieb es in seinen Tagebüchern von 1777 und 1778 und er legt Wert auf die Feststellung, daß, was er beobachtete, ein Zeitvertreib war, der in keiner Weise mit Arbeit verbunden war. 1821 wurde das Surfen jedoch von Missionaren, die es aufs heftigste mißbilligten, von Tahiti verbannt.

Der Begründer des Surfens im zwanzigsten Jahrhundert war der Fürst Paon Kahanamoku, der große Schwimmer aus Hawaii, der bei den Olympischen Spielen von 1912 und 1920 die 100 m im Freistilschwimmen gewann. Er reiste mit seinen Surfbrettern, langen, unhandlichen, schweren Dingern, in der Welt herum, und er ließ überall dort eines zurück, wo er glaubte, daß Surfen Fuß fassen könnte.

Polish up your grammar.

Notes on expressing future time.

1. To be going to + infinitive:

With a personal subject the meaning is: somebody definitely intends to do something.
Example: I don't like this hotel, I'm not going to stay here.

94

2. To be about to + infinitive:

It expresses **near** future.
Example: The train is about to leave. − (. . . wird **gleich** abfahren.)

3. To be to + infinitive:

This expresses a) a command
                b) an arrangement.

a) You are to work harder. − Du mußt härter arbeiten.
b) They are to be married in October.

4. Simple present:

Expresses a fixed programme.
Example: The play starts at seven p.m.

5. Present progressive:

Generally expresses the intention of the speaker or a plan. It nearly always requires a future time phrase.
Example: We're meeting there this evening.

Notes on modal "shall".

1. I | shall / will | try to do my best.

"Shall" is only used with **I** and **we** in formal British English.
"Will" is used in **all** persons in British and American English.

2. "Shall" cannot be replaced by "will" in questions in the first person. (Shall I help you?)

3. "Shall" is widely used to express intention in the first person. (We shall win some day. − I shall be back soon.)

4. "Shall" is used in the 2nd and 3rd persons to express:
a) insistence (You shall hand these papers to me.)
b) promise (They shall have the money.)

95

Notes on semi-auxiliaries.

John is | likely | to come.   – John kommt wahrscheinlich.
        | liable |

John is | certain | to come.   – John kommt gewiß/sicherlich.
        | sure |
        | bound |

John is unlikely to come.   – John kommt wahrscheinlich
                                   nicht.

5. Europe's Dying Forests

The disease strikes selectively but with deadly effect. In the case of a spruce tree, the branches at first hang limply, like Spanish moss. Between five weeks and three years later, the branches are tinged with yellow and then brown. The weakened tree soon drops its needles and
5 eventually stops growing new ones. It becomes bald at the top and appears stunted, spreading its highest branches outward and upward like a stork's nest. In a desperate struggle for life, it may grow excessive numbers of cones or sprout "anxiety shoots" — tiny branches that grow irregularly around the bough. Roots and trunks begin to twist
10 and shrink. Finally, drought, frost, insects and parasites finish off the weakened plant. In the end, it stands like a bony finger pointing toward the sky.

The epidemic of dying trees has swept through Europe as mercilessly as the Black Death did during the Middle Ages — and in ways that are
15 just as mysterious. The new plague hits young saplings as well as 120-year-old firs and strikes individual trees as frequently as whole forests. Even the course of the illness has been difficult to pinpoint. Death by *Waldsterben* was first thought to take two to three years. But some recently observed cases have taken only five weeks to develop.
20 "We used to clear out the dead wood every four years," says an owner of a small forest, "now we have to go through every year."

Explanations for the epidemic range from a cyclic change in the environment to a baffling form of tree "cancer". But the most convincing evidence points to air pollution, especially sulfur dioxide (SO_2)
25 and oxides of nitrogen (NO_2), which are spewed into the air by the ton from electrical generation plants, industrial boilers, smelting plants and automobiles.

What makes tracking down the cause of toxic poisoning so frustratingly difficult is the caprice of the wind. Modern smokestacks, rising more
30 than 1.200 ft., may spare the surrounding countryside. But they can emit pollutants high into the air, where they travel along wind-formed "skyways" that can carry them hundreds of miles, even beyond the country that produced them.

The most dramatic example of "pollution drift" comes from Great
35 Britain, which has the ignominious honour of being the largest
generator of SO_2 in Western Europe. A 1984 report by the environment committee of the House of Commons estimates that 28 % of the
5.1 million tons of sulfur dioxide belched from British smokestacks
each year are windborne to other countries, principally in Scandinavia.
40 According to Friends of the Earth, an international environmental
group, British emissions account for 14 % of the pollution in Sweden
and 7 % in both Norway and West Germany. Scandinavian scientists
claim that the resultant downpour of acid rain has already caused a
15 % decline in timber growth.

45 Whether a nation is a sinner or a victim tends to dictate its position on
international pollution standards. Those that are sinned against,
notably the Scandinavian countries, have worked for many years to
make acid rain an international issue. The sinners, like Britain, have
resisted putting teeth into pollution control regulations since they must
50 bear the costs but enjoy few of the benefits.

Many West Europeans, however, seem willing to pay more for products and services if they can be assured of healthy trees and clean air.
A poll released in July, 1985, when unemployment in most of the E.C.
stood at 11 % and inflation was at 8.5 % throughout the Community,
55 showed that nearly a third of Europeans were ready to accept higher
energy prices and a greater dependence on foreign imports to protect
the environment.

Indeed saving the rapidly deteriorating forests of Europe will probably
require an offensive campaign that includes a defensive scheme which
60 calls for reduction in toxic emissions. But it will require more money
than is currently being spent on such measures, as well as an overwean-
ing commitment to protecting the environment, even if the trade-off is
slower economic growth. "We must strive to make the air as clean as
technical possibilities allow, without considering the cost", says a
65 Munich University Researcher. "The destruction of nature is too high
a price to pay." Many of his fellow Europeans are beginning to agree.

I. Vocabulary

spruce (tree)	—	Fichte
to tinge	to give a slight degree of a colour to	färben, schattieren
limp	lacking strength or stiffness	schlaff, kraftlos
bald	with little or no hair	kahl
stunted	prevented from full growth	verkümmert, verkrüppelt
cone	fruit of a pine or fir	Zapfen
to sprout	to grow or come out	sprießen, keimen
drought [draut]	a long period of dry weather	Dürre, Trockenheit
merciless	willing to punish rather than to forgive	gnadenlos
the Black Death	the illness (the plague) that killed large numbers of people in Europe in the 14th century	die Pest
a sapling	a young tree	Bäumchen
to pinpoint	to find or describe the exact nature or cause	genau festlegen, bestimmen
to baffle	to make effective action impossible by confusing	verwirren
cancer	diseased growth in the body	Krebs(-krankheit)
sulfur (dioxide)	—	Schwefel(-dioxyd)
nitrogen	—	Stickstoff
to spew	to cause to come out in a rush or flood	ausspucken, auswerfen
to track down	to find by hunting or searching	aufspüren

toxic	poisonous	giftig
ignominious	causing strong public disapproval	schimpflich, schmählich, schändlich
environmental	(see: Pitfalls)	
acid rain	—	saurer Regen
timber	wood for building	Bauholz, Nutzholz
a poll	—	Meinungsumfrage
overweaning (fml)	exaggerated, excessive	übertrieben, exzessiv
commitment	responsibility	Verantwortung, Verpflichtung
trade-off	here: disadvantage resulting from a deal	hier: Nachteil, der aus einem Handel (Geschäft) entsteht

Pitfalls in the language

1. environmentalist   – Umweltschützer
   – a person who tries to prevent the environment from being spoilt;

   environment   – Umwelt
   – all the surrounding conditions which influence growth and development;

   surroundings   – Umgebung
   – the place which surrounds one;
   (We made an excursion into the surroundings of London.)

   – environmental protection (laws) – Umweltschutz (-gesetze)
   – ecology   – Ökologie; (Wissenschaft von den . . .) Beziehungen der Lebewesen zu ihrer Umwelt

2. disease (line 1)   – Krankheit
   The term "illness" (Krankheit) is not used when speaking of plants or animals.

   Pay special attention to the pronunciation and spelling:

   > disease [di'zi:z]
   > decease [di'si:s] (– Tod)

II. Questions

1. Describe the analogy between the current disease affecting forests and the Black Death in the Middle Ages. (See page 97)

2. Which explanations are there in the text for the dying of the trees? (Use your own words as far as possible.) (See page 100)

3. Give a critical analysis of Britain's attitude towards environmental concerns as expressed in the text. (See page 102)

4. What does the author want to stress by juxtaposing (1) the West Europeans' readiness to preserve their environment and the economic situation in the European Community?
   (1) to juxtapose – gegenüberstellen (See page 103)

5. Which suggestions are made in the last paragraph to stop forests from becoming extinct? (See page 106)

6. Find the essential ideas in each paragraph. (See page 108)

7. Composition: What measures should be taken in your eyes to prevent the dying of trees? (See page 108)

8. Translation (See page 110)

1. Describe the analogy between the current disease affecting forests and the Black Death in the Middle Ages.

We can establish an analogy between the disease of trees and the plague in the Middle Ages on several accounts: the plague spread rapidly through

Europe killing large numbers of people. At that time, there was no cure which could save infected people from death; young and old alike were helplessly left to that fate. In our times, vast areas of forests in Europe are falling victim to (1) the disease of trees. So far, no effective remedy (2) has been discovered to prevent forests suffering from this devastation (3).

(1) to fall victim to – zum Opfer fallen; (2) a remedy – ein Heilmittel; (3) devastation – Zerstörung

---

Note on stylistic devices: **analogy (Ähnlichkeit, Entsprechung, Analogie)**

An **analogy** is a resemblance in regard to some elements, characteristics, qualities, parts, etc., between things which are otherwise completely different from each other.

The stylistic device of analogy is used to achieve certain effects, for example, to **make something clear** to the reader, to **set** the reader **thinking**, or to **stir** the reader's **emotion**.

Expressing ideas: anlogy – Analogie

| to | draw
establish
build up | an analogy between (two things) |

| Something | is analogous to . . .
has its analogy in . . . |

| The analogy
between . . .
and . . . | reveals
elucidates

makes us
aware of | – *enthüllt*
– *gibt Auf-
schluß über*
– *macht uns
bewußt* | man's helplessness;
the devastation of . . .;
the seriousness of . . .;
etc. |

102

Word field: disease, illness − Krankheit

infirmity debility (fml)	− *Schwäche, Schwachheit, Gebrechen*
plague	− *Geißel, Plage, Seuche, Pest*
epidemic	− *(grassierende) Krankheit, Seuche, Epidemie*
infection	− *Ansteckung, Infektion*
contagion	− *Ansteckung (durch Berührung)*
infirm (fml)	− *schwach, hilflos*
decrepit	− *gebrechlich, hinfällig, altersschwach*
incurable	− *unheilbar*
mortally ill	− *todkrank*
to catch	− *sich zuziehen*
to suffer **from**	− *leiden* **an** a disease
to cure	− *heilen*
to show symptoms **of**	*Symptome, Anzeichen, Merkmale* **für** *etwas zeigen*
to languish	*darniederliegen, dahinsiechen*

Word field: decease, death − Tod

extinction	− *das Aussterben, die Vernichtung, das Auslöschen*
mortality	− *Sterblichkeit, Sterben*
death rate	− *Sterblichkeitsziffer*
mortal	− *sterblich, tödlich, todbringend*
fatal	− *tödlich*
deceased	− *verstorben*
lifeless	− *leblos*

to die **of** a disease	– **an** *einer Krankheit sterben*
to become extinct	– *aussterben*
to perish	– *umkommen (durch Unfall, Naturgewalt, Hunger usw.).*

2. Which explanations are there in the text for the dying of the trees? (Use your own words as far as possible.)

There are three explanations for the dying of the trees. (lines 22 – 27) Firstly, a regular rotation in the ecology, secondly, a deadly tree disease, and thirdly, the emission of toxical chemicals into the air.

Expressing ideas: 1. (causes of) pollution – Umweltverschmutzung

---

a) air pollution

Sulphur dioxide is a	toxic poisonous } – *giftig* noxious – *schädlich*		substance; chemical; element; material; etc.
Large quantities of this noxious element	are emitted by (– *werden ausgestoßen von*)	residential heating – (*Heizungen in Wohnhäusern*); power stations – (*Kraftwerke*); the burning of coal; etc.
This factory chemical power station	is a	pollutant – (*ein Schadstoff*) polluter – (*Zerstörer der Umwelt*)	

These environmental ills (*Umweltschäden*) are caused by the emission of . . . (e.g. car-exhaust fumes – *Autoabgase*).

104

b) water pollution

Factories, cities, etc.	dump	– (*einlassen*) poison into	the river;
	choke	– (*ersticken*)	the water of
	foul	– (*verschmutzen*)	our lakes.

---

2. effects of pollution

| Acid rain, chemicals, fertilizers, insecticides, etc. | threaten pose a threat to } – *bedrohen* | the environment. the landscape. human health. water purity (*Reinheit*). |

| People, forests, nature, etc. | is are | endangered by jeopardised by vulnerable **to** | – *gefährdet* – *verletzungs-anfällig* **für** | contamination. |

| Disastrous effects of pollution include | the destruction of forests; the fouling/contamination of rivers; the deterioration (– *Verschlechterung*) in people's health; water that is no longer potable (fml) /drinkable; serious damage to . . . (wild life); poisoned farmland; irreversible (– *nicht wieder gutzu-machen*) damage to . . . . |

People's life-expectancy (– *Lebenserwartung*) is shortened (by . . .)

3. Give a critical analysis of Britain's attitude towards environmental concerns as expressed in the text.

Great Britain produces a large quantity of harmful substances which pollute the air. The country, however, is in a favourable position; it does not suffer directly from these pollutants, since the prevailing winds drive them across the North Sea and the Channel to the Continent, especially to Scandinavia, causing pollution-related damage in these regions.

Despite these proven facts, Great Britain is – for financial reasons – unwilling to introduce stricter regulations to protect the environment of her neighbours. This attitude towards the world-wide concern for the environment is irresponsible.

Expressing ideas: 1. contrary – Gegenteil

This	attitude, behaviour, etc.	is	far from being anything but	– *weit entfernt von* – *alles andere als*	responsible.

This is	quite the contrary of . . . the very opposite of . . .	. . . *genau das Gegenteil von* . . .

Something is	the opposite the inverse the converse	– *Gegenteil*	of . . . .

On the contrary (– **im** *Gegenteil*) the British do not feel responsible for . . . .

106

2. contrast — Gegensatz

Something	contrasts **with** is a contrast **to** is **in** contrast **to** } — *steht im Gegensatz zu* . . . is the other extreme of . . .
In contrast	with Great Britain, the Scandinavian countries . . . to

By contrast, other countries fight against . . . (*Im Gegensatz dazu* . . .)
Contrary to Great Britain, other countries . . .

Note:

The use of "**on the contrary**" and "**in contrast**"

Use "on the contrary" if you want to assert that the opposite of a stated fact is actually true.

Example:

Some experts maintain that our forests will survive. On the contrary, they will probably disappear in the near future.

Use "in contrast to" if you want to say that two things are very different.

Example:

In contrast to all European countries, there is no speed limit on German motorways.

4. What does the author want to stress by juxtaposing (1) the West Europeans' readiness to preserve their environment and the economic situation in the European Community?

   (1) to juxtapose — nebeneinanderstellen

107

The author's intention is to emphasize the extent of the West Europeans' environmental concern. Despite high unemployment and inflation rates, they are prepared to lower their standard of living to help save the eviromment. Many West Europeans have developed a new sense of responsibility. As the poll indicates, nearly a third are of the opinion that money should be rather spent for the perservation of nature than for giving a new impetus (1) to the economy. In their view, it is an unpolluted environment that ranks higher.

(1) impetus – Anstoß

Expressing ideas: to stress something – etwas betonen, hervorheben

---

The author,	stresses/emphasizes	– *betont,*	the fact
The text,	lays the stress on	*hebt*	that . . .
This argument,		*hervor*	
This comparison,	lays the emphasis on		
This juxtaposition,			
etc.			

Note on developing your writing skills:

When you answer comprehension questions or when you write a composition you should try to lay the emphasis on what you think is important.

Example:

Trees suffer most from air pollution. — **It is the trees that** suffer most from air pollution.

Here are some useful ways to give weight to your arguments:

1. How to stress nouns and noun phrases:
   a) the subject of a sentence:

The Prime Minister should make a decision.	**It is the Prime Minister who** should make a decision.
The quality of our drinking water deteriorates more and more.	**It is the quality of our drinking water that** deteriorates more and more.

   b) the object or prepositional object of a sentence:

Polluting factories should install filters.	**It is filters that** polluting factories should install.
The Greens are fighting for lead-free petrol.	**It is for lead-free petrol that** the Greens are fighting.

The adjective "**very**" can also be used to give weight to nouns:

The costs of the catalytic converter *(Katalysator)* are too high.	The **very costs** of the catalytic converter are too high.
These measures must be effected immediately.	These **very measures** must be effected immediately.

Another stylistic device for stressing nouns is the use of emphasizing pronouns with **-self**:

Man destroys nature.	**Man himself** destroys nature.
Nature is in danger.	**Nature itself** is in danger.

2. How to stress verbs and verb phrases:
   a) with the auxiliary "**do**":

Lead-free fuel reduces air pollution.	Lead-free fuel **does reduce** air pollution.

b) with adverbs:

We must find a solution to this problem.	We must	certainly definitely truly clearly indeed	find a solution to this problem.

5. Which suggestions are made in the last paragraph to stop forests from becoming extinct? (Use your own words as far as is appropriate.)

Society must definitely spare no efforts to decrease the pollution of the environment. More money must be invested in pollution-reducing devices, even if our economy thus grows at a slower pace. Everyone must make it his very duty to contribute to the solution of this ecological problem.

Word field: 1. to make an effort to do something − sich bemühen, sich anstrengen, etwas zu tun

---

to spare no effort to do something − keine Mühe scheuen

to make	an endeavour an effort	to do something

to strive	− *sich bemühen*	
to seek	− *suchen, versuchen*	
to struggle	− *kämpfen*	for something
to try one's best	− *sein Bestes tun*	to do something
to do one's utmost	− *sein Äußerstes tun*	

110

2. a) responsibility – Verantwortung

a sense of respon-sibility	– *Verantwortungs-gefühl*
to take full respon-sibility for	– *die volle Verant-wortung auf sich nehmen für . . .*
to blame for	– *verantwortlich machen für . . ./zur Verantwortung ziehen wegen . . .*

| It is | our the politicians' everybody's | responsibility duty commitment obligation | – *Verantwortung* – *Pflicht* – *Verpflichtung* | to save our forests. |

| We should We ought to | make it our duty to commit ourselves to engage ourselves **to** | – *. . . uns zur Pflicht machen . . .* – *. . . uns verpflichten zu . . .* – *. . . uns einsetzen **für** . . .* |

| It is **up** to | us, everybody, etc. | to . . . . | – *Es ist unsere Aufgabe, . . . Es liegt an uns, . . .* |

b) irresponsibility – Unverantwortlichkeit

| The use of too many insecticides and pesticides | is | irresponsible. (– *unverantwortlich*) inexcusable. (– *nicht zu entschuldigen*) unjustifiable. (– *nicht zu rechtfertigen*) |

6. Find the essential ideas in each paragraph.

1 st: The author describes a tree caught in the gradual process of decay and death.

2 nd: A comparison with the Black Death of the Middle Ages is given; the speed with which the disease spreads is thus made clear.

3 rd: The author lists several reasons for the dying of the trees, of which air pollution is the most plausible. (1)

4 th: It is difficult to find the causes of pollution in one country because prevailing winds carry pollutants far from their sources.

5 th: Britain's emissions are driven to Scandinavia and the Continent and hardly affect Britain at all.

6 th: Conflicting views on pollution are apparent: Great Britain is unwilling to take effective steps in the matter, whereas the Scandinavian countries have long been active in this field.

7 th: West Europeans are ready to lower their standard of living in order to preserve the environment.

8 th: More commitment – both in ideal and financial terms – is necessary to reduce air pollution and thus save nature.

   (1) plausible – glaubhaft

7. Composition: What measures should be taken in your eyes to prevent the dying of trees?

In my opinion, it is the government, industry and the individual that are called upon to take measures to hinder the extinction of our forests; for only a concerted effort (1) of all those responsible will enable us to avoid a catastrophe.

In the first place, it is up to the government to pass stringent (2) environmental legislation and to see to it that such laws are enforced, if necessary by means of hefty fines (3). It is also the government's job to promote international co-operation so that polluter countries such as Great Britain are made to see the irresponsibility of their laxity in environmental matters.

Secondly, industries that pollute the environment should do all in their power to reduce their emissions without waiting for the government or the courts to force them. The installation of filters and pollution-reducing devices — perhaps financially supported by the taxpayer — as well as a reduction in the use of fossil fuels and toxic chemicals would be two useful ways of preventing pollution by industry.

Thirdly, the individual, too, has an obligation to do whatever he or she can to eliminate the killing of our forests. One useful method is the purchase and installation of a catalytic converter for automobiles. This device — in combination with lead-free (4) petrol and a self-imposed speed limit on motorways — represent a direct and active contribution to relieving (5) the strain on our forests.

On another level, it is also necessary to support environmental groups and political parties advocating protection of nature; in this way pressure can be put on political institutions and a new public awareness of ecological problems can be fostered (6).

(1) concerted effort — gemeinsame/aufeinander abgestimmte
                        Bemühungen
(2) stringent — streng, scharf, hart
(3) hefty fines — beträchtliche/hohe Geldstrafen
(4) lead-free — or: unleaded — bleifrei
(5) to relieve — erleichtern, entlasten
(6) to foster — fördern

8. Translation

A Dying Landscape

Not long ago, most East European governments dismissed environmental pollution as a capitalist problem. In communist countries, they argued, the lack of a profit motive did away with the main cause for industrial pollution, and governments could use their ownership of factories to impose uniform purity standards. While the argument was ingenious, it turned out to be dead wrong. Over the past two decades, pollution has turned the East European landscape into a disaster zone of dying forests, poisoned farmland, crumbling cities and noxious rivers. Today the environment is an explosive social and political issue in every country of the Eastern bloc.

One cause of the problem is East Europe's cramped geography. Unlike the Soviet Union and the United States, where vast land masses can absorb a good deal of pollution with relative ease, the countries of Central and Eastern Europe are squeezed into a narrow, heavily populated corridor. Clouds heavy with acid rain drift across borders, while a complex river system carries tainted water from one nation to the next. The most heavily polluted countries – East Germany, Czechoslovakia, Poland and Hungary – all rely on high-sulfur lignite coal as a primary energy source. They lack adequate water-filtration facilities, while the populations of their major cities have doubled since World War II. Their small, cheap cars have no antipollutant equipment, and their modern agriculture is overdependent on high-phosphorus chemical fertilizers that eventually reduce crop yields.

Vocabulary

to dismiss as	to put away (a subject) from one's mind	über etwas hinweg-gehen, etwas abtun als
ingenious	having or showing cleverness at inventing things	klug, kunstvoll, er-finderisch (angelegt)
disaster	a sudden great misfortune	Unglück, Katastrophe
cramped	limited in space	beengt, eng

114

to taint	to spoil, make unfit for use	unbrauchbar/ ungenießbar machen, verderben
lignite coal	—	Braunkohle
yield	that which is produced as a fruit or profit	Ertrag, Gewinn

Sterbende Landschaften

Noch vor kurzer Zeit taten die meisten osteuropäischen Regierungen die Umweltverschmutzung als ein Problem der kapitalistischen Länder ab. Sie behaupteten, daß es in kommunistischen Ländern keinen Ansporn gebe, Profit zu machen, und daß deshalb die Hauptursache industrieller Umweltverschmutzung gar nicht besteht. Die Regierungen könnten, weil sie Besitzer der Fabriken sind, einheitliche Richtlinien zur Reinhaltung der Umwelt erlassen. Dieses Argument war zwar klug gewählt, es war jedoch, wie sich herausstellte, absolut falsch. Während der letzten zwei Jahrzehnte hat die Umweltverschmutzung die osteuropäische Landschaft in ein Katastrophengebiet verwandelt, in der Wälder sterben, Äcker und Flüsse vergiftet sind und die Häuser in den Städten langsam verfallen. Heute ist das Thema 'Umwelt' in jedem Ostblockland ein gesellschaftlicher und politischer Diskussionspunkt, der viel 'Sprengstoff' enthält.

Eine Ursache des Problems liegt darin, daß die Länder Osteuropas auf kleinem Raum eng aneinandergrenzen. Hierin unterscheiden sie sich von der Sowjetunion und den Vereinigten Staaten, wo riesige Gebiete einen großen Teil der Verschmutzung aufnehmen können. Die Länder Mittel- und Osteuropas liegen eng zusammengedrängt in einem schmalen, dicht bevölkerten Korridor. Wolken, die große Mengen an saurem Regen mit sich führen, können (ungehindert) über die Grenzen treiben; ein weitver-zweigtes Flußsystem führt gleichzeitig stark verschmutztes Wasser von einer Nation zur anderen. Die Länder mit der höchsten Umweltverschmut-zung − die DDR, die Tschechoslowakei, Polen und Ungarn − sind alle abhängig von stark schwefelhaltiger Braunkohle als ihre wichtigste Energiequelle. Ihnen fehlen entsprechende Anlagen, um das Wasser zu filtrieren, während sich die Einwohnerzahlen ihrer bedeutendsten Städte seit dem Ende des Zweiten Weltkrieges verdoppelt haben. Ihre kleinen, billigen Autos sind nicht umweltfreundlich ausgestattet, und ihre moderne Landwirtschaft ist viel zu abhängig von chemischen Düngemitteln mit hohem Phosphoranteil, die unter Umständen die Ernteerträge verringern können.

Polish Up Your Grammar

Inversion (Change of word order)

Text: "...", says a Munich University Researcher, "...". (Line 64)

In sentences with "to say" (or verbs with a similar meaning) appended to a direct quotation, the subject may follow the verb. (Exception: the subject is a personal pronoun.)

Note on style:

In formal (or literary) English the word order "Subject – Verb" is changed to "Verb – Subject" if a sentence begins with "negative" or "restrictive" expressions.

Inversion of this kind creates an **emphatic** and **emotional** tone.

Example:

Ordinary tone: Emphatic tone:

Europe's forests have never been   **Never** have Europe's forests been
threatened to such an extent.   threatened to such an extent.

Examples of **negative/restrictive** expressions:

Nowhere has anything like this been experienced before.
Seldom/Rarely can we find symptoms of improvement.

116

Hardly had they discovered the cause of the problem, when they realized it was too late to save the environment.

Here are some useful phrases to begin your sentences. They **always** require inverted word order.

On no account must we abandon our forests. − Auf keinen Fall dürfen wir unsere Wälder aufgeben.

On no occasion did they deviate from their plan. − Bei keiner Gelegenheit wichen sie von ihrem Plan ab.

Under no circumstances must we give up the fight. − Unter keinen Umständen dürfen wir den Kampf aufgeben.

Only by this means is it possible to save the rivers. − Nur durch dieses Mittel (diese Maßnahme) ist es möglich . . .

6. An embarrassment of colas

The year 1985 takes up a disproportionate share of the "Concise History of Coca-Cola", which is as follows:

1886, John Pemberton, an Atlanta druggist, mixes sweet concoction to secret formula, which combined with soda water becomes Coca-Cola.

5 1923, Robert Woodruff becomes president of Coca-Cola Company.

1985 (March), Robert Woodruff dies.

1985 (April), Coke's chairman, Roberto Goizueta, responding to Coke's loss of market share, scraps Coke's old formula and introduces new Coke.

1985 (July), Roberto Goizueta, responding to popular demand, brings back old Coke,
10 now known as Coca-Cola Classic.

One or two events are missing from the concise history − for instance, how Coke became the world's best-selling soft drink, thanks in part to Woodruff's skill during the second world war in making Coca-Cola available to every American serviceman abroad for just a nickel a bot-
15 tle. The concise history also fails to describe how Coca-Cola came to be an American institution, a symbol of American vigour, an instrument of foreign policy sent in more often and perhaps with more effect than the marines, a synonym for corporate success and for many years the economic mainstay of Atlanta. Woodruff, who formally gave up
20 running the company in 1955, remained its most powerful, albeit unseen, presence, until his death at 95 this year. His wishes and his cheque-book decided issues as various as Martin Luther King's funeral and Emory University's health sciences centre; he gave away, it is reckoned, about $350m, perhaps $200m of it to Emory.

25 He also, it has been said, latterly had an enervating effect on the
management of Coca-Cola. For although before his death Coke had
begun to diversify into many products, notably wine (it bought Taylor
in 1977 but sold its wine division in 1983 for what it paid for it) and
films (it bought Columbia Pictures in 1982), it had failed to hold its
30 share of the softdrinks market. Pepsi-Cola was making inroads at
home, particularly in supermarkets, where it overtook Coke in 1977.
Pepsi, boosted by clever advertising — "the Pepsi generation" and
Michael Jackson — appealed to the young, whose importance as consumers of sweet soft drinks has grown commensurately with older
35 Americans' concern about their waistlines (yuppy tummy). Abroad,
where Coke sells more than half its fizzy drinks and generates more
than 60 % of its earnings, growth had also been too slow.

However, the decision to improve performance not by marketing but
by changing the formula — "one of the easiest we ever made", said
Mr. Goizueta at the time — seemed to some people an act of
40 astonishing foolhardiness. The change was justified by tests among
more than 200 000 consumers, a majority of whom liked the new taste;
and advice on selling the new product was taken from experts as
diverse as Mr Pat Caddell, the Democratic pollster, and Mr Richard
45 Wirthlin, the consultant to President Reagan and other Republicans.
But many were sceptical, even without knowing that those tested had
not been told that a vote for the new Coke meant the death of the old
Coke.

Had not Schlitz, after all, shown the dangers of taking liberties with
50 taste buds? In 1974, having been America's second most popular beer,
it changed its brewing technique, only to see its market share collapse.
Coca-Cola, it was said, was now daring to touch the untouchable —
the 7X formula — and risked destroying the mystique that was its most
precious asset. Bets were placed that Mr Goizueta would not last
55 another year as chairman, and that an outside director such as Mr
James Williams, president of the Trust Company of Georgia, Coca-
Cola's bank, would take over.

That looks less likely now that the loyalist rebellion has penetrated the
Coke boardroom and won a reprieve for the old formula. For Coke,
60 more by luck than by design, seems to have a winning combination on

its hands. With the old and the new Cokes, it has both "the real thing" and something else that tastes to many remarkably like Pepsi. Add to that Cherry Coke, diet Coke, caffeine-free Coke, caffeine-free diet Coke, Tab and caffeine-free Tab, not to speak of Sprite, Fanta, Mello
65 Yello, etc., and Coke has something for everybody (well, a lot of people). At present shareholders and analysts seem happy, though some worry that such an embarrassment of colas will cause marketing problems about which to promote and lead retailers to drop one in favour of another. For the time being, however, Mr Woodruff can stop turning in his grave.

I. Vocabulary

embarrassment	feeling of perplexity	Verwirrung, Bestürzung
disproportionate	too large or too small, out of proportion	unverhältnismäßig
share	part belonging to (a person, firm, etc.)	Anteil
concoction	—	Getränk, Gebräu
druggist (AmE)	chemist, pharmacist	Apotheker
chairman	here: person directing a big firm	Vorsitzender, Präsident
to respond to	1. to answer 2. to act in answer to	1. beantworten 2. reagieren auf
to scrap	to throw away as useless or worn out	wegwerfen, ausrangieren
concise	giving much information in few words	knapp, präzise
available	something that may be obtained, got, etc.	erhältlich, verfügbar
service man	member of the army/navy/air force	Soldat

nickel	US coin worth 5 cents	Fünfcentstück
to fail	here: to neglect, to omit	versäumen, unterlassen
vigour	strength, forcefulness	Kraft, Energie
a marine (AmE)	—	Marineinfanterist
corporate	belonging to a group/body	vereinigt, zu einer Körperschaft/Firma gehörend
mainstay	chief means of support	wichtigste (Haupt-) Stütze
albeit (fml)	although, even though	obgleich, obwohl
issue	here: important point	Kernpunkt
to reckon	to suppose, to guess	vermuten, meinen, schätzen
to enervate	to cause to lose strength	schwächen
to diversify	here: to make different sorts of products	die Produktion um verschiedene Waren erweitern
to make inroads	to advance suddenly into a new area	hier: plötzlich Marktanteile gewinnen
to boost (coll.)	to help to advance or improve	fördern, unterstützen
commensurately	in the right proportion to/with	im Einklang mit, entsprechend
yuppy	(See note below.)	
tummy (coll.)	stomach	hier: Bäuchlein
fizzy	producing bubbles	schäumend
foolhardiness	taking of unwise risks	Tollkühnheit
(opinion) poll	—	Meinungsumfrage

pollster	—	Meinungsforscher
consultant	person giving specialist or professional advice to others	Berater
to take liberties (with)	to set aside conventions/ rules	sich Freiheiten herausnehmen (gegenüber)
taste buds	—	Geschmacksnerven der Zunge
Schlitz	(See note below.)	
asset	here: valuable quality	Wert, Vorzug
boardroom	room for meetings of the directors of a company	Sitzungssaal
a reprieve	giving relief for a short time (from danger, etc.)	Gnadenfrist, Aufschub, Atempause
shareholder	owner of shares	Aktionär
to promote	here: to advertise	werben für
retailer	person selling products directly to consumers	Einzelhändler, Wiederverkäufer

Notes:
yuppy

This term is an **acronym**, i.e. it is made up of the first letters of "**y**oung **u**rban **p**rofessional". It denotes a person, male or female, holding a well-paid position, who is ambitious to climb up the social ladder. He or she pursues an exclusive lifestyle which reveals itself in elegant clothes, stylish homes, trendy cars and extravagant leisure activities.

Other acronyms: UNO, Nato, USA, etc.

Schlitz: Big US concern brewing beer;
Michael Jackson: famous pop singer

Pitfalls in the vocabulary of the text.

1. concise — kurz, prägnant, knapp
   a concise report/speech/
   article, etc.

   precise — genau, korrekt, richtig,
   präzise
   precise statistics, a precise
   mind, etc.

2. vigour
   (vigorous)
   — Kraft, Vitalität, Energie, Stärke,
   the vigour of an idea/a person/a
   firm/a country, etc.

   rigour
   (rigorous)
   — Schärfe, Strenge, Unerbittlichkeit
   the rigour of the law/of winter/of
   the fight

Pay special attention to the different meanings of:

1. to appeal to . . . (for . . .)
   a) jemanden bitten um
      to appeal to someone for help/sup-
      port, etc.

   b) jemandem gefallen, angezogen sein
      von
      This girl/boy/film/book appeals to
      me.

   c) ansprechen, appellieren an
      This author appeals to society's
      responsibility for the poor.

2. concern **of** . . .
   a) Sache, Angelegenheit
      That is no concern **of** mine.

124

concern **for**	b) Sorge, Beunruhigung His concern **for** the future is . . .
concern	c) Firma The concern makes a lot of profit from . . .
to concern	– betreffen, angehen This problem concerns everybody.
to be concerned **about**	– besorgt sein um People are concerned about inflation.

II. Questions.

1. What is known about the composition of Coca-Cola? (See p. 122)

2. For what reasons does the year 1985 take up a "disproportionate share" of the "Concise History of Coca-Cola"? (See p. 123)

3. Describe Robert Woodruff's achievement as president of the Coca-Cola company. (See p. 125)

4. Which factors helped Pepsi-Cola to make a breakthrough in the soft-drinks market? (See p. 126)

5. Was Robert Goizueta's decision to change the formula of Coca-Cola based on good reason? (See p. 129)

6. a) Draw a parallel between "Schlitz" and the Coca-Cola company's experience with the new beer and coke. (See p. 130)

   b) What does the negative question "Had not Schlitz, after all, shown . . .?" (line 49) imply? (See p. 132)

7. Summarize the text from line 25 to 37. (See p. 133)

8. Composition: Discuss the role of advertising in Western society. (See p. 133)

9. Translate.

1. What is known about the composition of Coca-Cola?

Coca-Cola consists of (1) soda water and a mixture of various ingredients: sugar, caffeine, and a substance called the "7 X formula" which is known only to a few. The trade name "Coca-Cola" suggests that it contains extracts from the coca bush and the cola nut.

(1)   to consist **of**   – bestehen **aus**
                                 Beer consists mainly **of** hops, malt and water.

        to consist **in**   – beruhen **auf**
                                 The popularity of this drink consists **in** its sweet flavour.

Word field: to be in/to be part of, etc. – enthalten, usw.

---

to contain   – *enthalten*
                    This report contains all the important facts.
                    One bottle contains one pint (= 0,57 l.) of beer.

to comprise   – *umfassen, einschließen*
                    The Republic of Eire (Irland) comprises three provinces: Leinster, Munster and Connaught.

to include   – *einschließen*
                    This price for the room includes a continental breakfast.
                    Inclusive of/including (tax) – *einschließlich (Steuer)*

to consist of   – *bestehen aus*
                    The new cabinet consists of twenty ministers.

2. For what reasons does the year 1985 take up a "disproportionate share" of the "Concise History of Coca-Cola?"

The "Concise History" mentions only two events in the long history of Coca-Cola from 1886 till 1984.
There are, however, three entries (1) for 1985 alone. The death of Robert Woodruff, the introduction of new Coke and the return to Coca-Cola classic mark are important events in the history of this soft drink.

(1) entry   − Eintrag
                 to make an entry in a list; a dictionary entry

---

Word field: a) event − Ereignis

---

event   − *(wichtiges) Ereignis*
                   This event changed the course of history.

incident
occurrence   } − *Vorfall, Zwischenfall, Vorkommnis, Ereignis*

                   Have you heard about this strange incident?
                   An incident on the border − *ein Grenzzwischenfall*

happening   − *(künstlerisches/politisches) Ereignis, das spontan oder*
                   mit wenig Planung/Organisation zustandekommt;
                   The passers-by were asked to take part in the happening.

---

b) to happen, etc. − sich ereignen usw.

---

to happen   }
to occur   }   − *sich ereignen*
                   The incident happened/occurred two weeks ago.

to happen **to**   − *jemandem passieren*
                   I'm afraid something has happened to him.

to chance
to happen to ⎫
(+ infinitive) ⎬ – *sich zufällig ereignen, sich ergeben*
I chanced/happened to be at home when she arrived.

to take place – *stattfinden*
When did the meeting take place?

Expressing ideas: developments – Entwicklungen

This year, | marks | the beginning of ⎫
event, | | the starting point of ⎬ – *Beginn*
plan, |
etc. | | the rise of ⎫
| | the growth of ⎬ – *Anstieg,*
| | the increase of ⎭ *Anwachsen*

the heyday of ⎫
the culmination of ⎬
the summit of ⎬ – *Höhepunkt*
the climax of ⎭

the turning point of – *Wendepunkt*

the decline of   – *Niedergang,*
the decrease of   – *Abnahme*
the diminution of   – *Verringerung*

the final stage of   – *das letzte*
                              Stadium
the end of   – *Schluß, Ende*

3. Describe Robert Woodruff's achievement as president of the Coca-Cola company.

The president accomplished the highest sales figures by making almost the whole world a market for this soft drink. The marketing tactics he used to reach this aim consisted in providing US servicemen with Coca-Cola at a low price in every part of the world, where they were stationed.

Word field: skill — Fähigkeit

---

skill	
ability	— *Fähigkeit, Geschicklichkeit, Können*

Ⅴ a skilled worker — *Facharbeiter, angelernter Arbeiter*
. a skilful worker — *ein geschickter, fähiger Arbeiter*

an unskilled worker — *Hilfsarbeiter, ungelernter Arbeiter*

aptitude
capacity — *angeborene Fähigkeit*
He shows great capacity/ability for dealing with people.

craft — *(handwerkliche) Fähigkeit, Geschicklichkeit*
the craft of a watch-maker

dexterity — *Fingerfertigkeit, Geschick*
the dexterity of a violinist

mastery — *Beherrschung*
His mastery of the piano is astonishing.

art — *Kunstfertigkeit, Kunst*
the art of photography
the art of dealing with people

Expressing ideas: cause and effect — Ursache und Wirkung

a) cause: The sales figures rose | on account of | his great skill.
	because of	
	thanks to	
	due to	
	owing to	

b) effect, result:

as a result of
— *wegen*
The firm went bankrupt as a result of bad management.

with the result that
— *mit dem Ergebnis, daß* . . .
Pepsico hired Michael Jackson with the result that sales rose sharply.

resultant (adj.)
— *sich daraus ergebend*
He worked day and night and the resultant profit made him a millionaire

to result **from**
— *sich ergeben aus*
His success results from talent and hard work.

to result **in**
— *führen zu*
The government's policy resulted in the creation of new jobs.

to result
(used intransitively)
— *(daraus) entstehen*
If they do not obey his orders, chaos will result.

4. Which factors helped Pepsi-Cola to make a breakthrough in the soft-drinks market?

Pepsi-Cola came to the fore (1) as a result of an efficient advertising campaign aimed at young people. For this purpose, Michael Jackson, a pop star adored (2) by hundreds of thousands of teenagers was hired by the public relations experts of Pepsi. Moreover, older Americans had drastically reduced their consumption (3) of Coca-Cola for fear of getting too fat, and a fatish appearance would also clearly disharmonize with the Yuppies' concept of sportiness.

The main reason, however, was the changing of the formula of Coca-Cola; the new one was not to the taste of (4) the consumers, who henceforth (5) tended to choose Pepsi rather than Coke.

(1) to come to the fore	in den Vordergrund treten
(2) to adore	verehren, anbeten
(3) consumption	Verbrauch, Verzehr, Konsum
(4) to be to the taste of	nach jemandes Geschmack sein
(5) henceforth	von da an, künftig

Word field: to hire − anwerben; mieten

---

to hire something	− *ausleihen, mieten (gegen Bezahlung)*
to hire out	− *vermieten (durch den Besitzer)*
to hire somebody (infml)	− *jemanden (kurzfristig) anstellen, einstellen*

to rent/hire a car	− *mieten*
to rent a house/an apartment/a flat	− *mieten*
to lease a car/a house	− *mieten*

to let a house/a flat	− *vermieten*

to lend someone something	− **an** *jemanden ausleihen* to lend a friend money
to borrow from	− **von** *jemandem ausleihen* to borrow money from a friend

Word field: advertising – Werbung

Advertising	highlights	– *(herausstellen)*	
	spotlights	– *(ins Scheinwerferlicht stellen)*	a product.
	boosts	– *(ankurbeln)*	

Advertising	*aims at/is aimed at*	– *(zielen auf)*	
	is directed at	– *(gerichtet an)*	consumers'
	appeals to	– *(ansprechen)*	wishes.

Advertising	manipulates	– *(manipulieren)*	
	persuades	– *(überreden)*	
	convinces	– *(überzeugen)*	
	wins over	– *(gewinnen)*	the
	allures	– *(anlocken)*	consumer.
	tempts	– *(verführen)*	

Note:

"**Ad**" (informal) is the short form for "advertisement". Informal words
of this kind are called **clippings** (to clip – to cut off).

Further examples of clippings:

bus	from	omnibus
flue		influenza (Grippe)
info		information
fab		fabulous (fabelhaft)
mike		microphone
fridge		refrigerator

132

5. Was Roberto Goizueta's decision to change the formula of Coca-Cola based on good reason?

Mr Goizueta was encouraged to produce a new Coke by specialists who had made a name for themselves as professional advisers for politicians. Besides, more than two hundred thousand people were selected to give their opinion about the new taste, and the majority of these testers considered it good.

Others, however, doubted the success of the new taste. Their distrust would have been greater if they had known that the testers had not been informed previously (1) that the production of the new Coke was tantamount to (2) the abandonment of (3) the old one.

Still others considered the change an unnecessary risk, and, indeed, the sales rates of the new Coke dropped to such an extent that R.G.'s position as chairman was undermined.

(1) previously   — zuvor
(2) to be tantamount to   — gleichbedeutend sein mit
(3) abandonment   — Preisgabe, Aufgabe

Word field: a) to judge — beurteilen, halten für

---

to evaluate   — *den Wert bestimmen*
to estimate   — *schätzen, berechnen,*
                 beurteilen
to measure   — *(ab-)schätzen*
measured by   — *gemessen an*
to be judged by — *gemessen werden an*
(one's deeds, not one's words)

b) to misjudge – falsch beurteilen

to overrate	
to overestimate	$\}$ – *überschätzen*
to overvalue	

to underrate	
to underestimate	$\}$ – *unterschätzen*
to undervalue	

not to do justice to a person/thing – *einer Sache/Person nicht gerecht werden*

6. a) Draw a comparison between the experience Schlitz had made and the Coca-Cola company's experience with the new beer and Coke.

In 1974, Schlitz, the second biggest brewery in the US, had changed its manner of producing beer which consequently altered its flavour. Thereby the consumers' preference for the old taste was not taken into consideration. The consumers were not willing to accept the new beer, and the sales plummeted.

Eleven years later, the Coca-Cola management made the same mistake by producing a new Coke with a slightly different taste. The results were similar to those of Schlitz.

Word field: a) comparison – Vergleich

to parallel with	
to compare with/to	$\}$ – *vergleichen*
to juxtapose	– *nebeneinander stellen*
to draw a comparison with	– *einen Vergleich ziehen*
compared with	– *verglichen mit*
in comparison with	– *im Vergleich zu*
comparable with/to	– *vergleichbar mit*
beyond compare	
incomparable	$\}$ – *unvergleichbar*

134

b) sameness – Gleichheit

sameness
identity $\Big\}$ – *Gleichheit*
exact likeness

same as
identical with $\Big\}$ – *gleich*
exactly alike

c) similarity – Ähnlichkeit

similarity with
resemblance between $\Big\}$ – *Ähnlichkeit*
similitude (lit.) with

similar to
like $\Big\}$ – *ähnlich*
resembling

to resemble
to look like $\Big\}$ – *ähnlich sein*

d) difference – Unterschied

the difference between — *Unterschied zwischen*

dissimilarity
disparity $\Big\}$ — *Verschiedenheit, Verschiedenartigkeit*

different from
unlike
distinct from $\Big\}$ — *verschieden, unterschiedlich*
dissimilar to

disparate — *ungleichartig*

distinguishable	– *unterscheidbar*

⚠	to differ **from**	– *sich unterscheiden von*
	to differ **in**	– *sich unterscheiden in*
	to differ **as to**	– *sich unterscheiden im Hinblick auf*

to differentiate between	– *einen Unterschied feststellen/sehen*
to make/draw a distinction between	*zwischen*

Expressing ideas: comparing – vergleichen

If we make a comparison between . . . and . . .	– we can say that . .
If we draw a parallel between . . . and . . .	– it becomes clear . .
	– it must be ad- mitted . . .
	etc.

Pepsi was more successful **in comparison with** Coke.

Pepsi's sales are not **comparable to** those of Coke.

Pepsi **stands/bears comparison with** . . . *(. . . hält den Vergleich mit*
. . . aus)

6. b) What does the negative question "Had not Schlitz, after all, shown . . ?" (Line 49) imply?

Using a negative question the author indirectly expresses his surprise that the failure of Schlitz's measures should not have been a lesson to Coke's managers.

(1) to imply – bedeuten, besagen, andeuten

136

> **Note:**
>
> Negative questions are often used to express **surprise** or **disbelief**.
>
> This type of questions may also express **annoyance** (Verärgerung) as in: "Why don't you stop talking?"

7. Summarize the text from line 25 to line 37.
   ("He also, it has been said . . . – also been too slow".)

Woodruff is said to have weakened the position of the company. Despite expansion and diversification into other areas, Coca-Cola was unable to defend its share of the soft-drinks market against Pepsi. The latter had won many customers away from Coke thanks to a clever advertising campaign aimed at the young. Moreover, foreign sales of Coke, which account for over half of the company's earnings, had stagnated.

8. Composition

Discuss the role of advertising in Western society.

Advertising, though totally absent in Eastern bloc countries, is omnipresent in the West and can thus be seen as a typical feature of Western capitalist societies. The necessity of advertising in a market based on competition must not be overlooked, but it is important to recognize that modern advertising is quite removed from its original aim of promoting a product to increase sales. Advertising has, in effect, become an end in itself and no longer plays a purely supportive role. Nowadays, the differences between various products – e.g. washing powders – are so minimal that it is the task of advertising to find, or better, invent aspects which make one product 'better' than its competitors. Real improvements, such as biodegradable and phosphate-free washing powders, are rare enough: for the most part, however, advertising relies on gimmicks, on catchy slogans or on the endorsement of celebrities. This has led to a lack of truth in

advertising since the truth — e.g. that there is little or no difference between various brands of washing powder — will not sell the product.
Through a constant barrage of advertising consumers, too, have been con-
ditioned not to look for facts or truth in advertising, but to react
favourably to a new package or 'fresher fragrance'.

That advertising has no longer a merely supportive function can be seen
in the advertising budgets of large firms. Millions of dollars are poured into advertising departments of large firms or are left at the advertising agen-
cies by smaller companies. The astronomical costs of advertising,
particularly of television commercials, lead to higher prices for the product
itself.

Although it is difficult to imagine our society without advertising, it may
be worth considering whether consumers would in fact rather forego advertising than pay higher prices for goods.

9. Translation

Coke Gives Soda-Pop Politics a New Twist

Note:

President	Term	President's party	Supporter of
Lyndon B. Johnson	1963 – 69	Dem.	Coca-Cola
Richard M. Nixon	1969 – 74	Rep.	Pepsi-Cola
Gerald R. Ford	1974 – 76	Rep.	Pepsi-Cola
Jimmy Carter	1976 – 80	Dem.	Coca-Cola
Ronald Reagan	1980 –	Rep.	Pepsi-Cola

With all the hoopla about the escalating cola war, one topic has been ignored: the political implications.

As with the political parties, there are only two major players: Coca-Cola,
the drink of Democrats, and Pepsi-Cola, the Republicans' refresher. Sure,
there are third-party colas, but as in politics not much is said about them.

This soda-pop politics is not coincidence. Coca-Cola has been the undisputed majority cola since the New Deal: The cola connection was formed in 1932, when the Democratic National Chairman Postmaster General James Farley, left the administration to become chairman of the Coca-Cola Export Corp. He had quarreled with Franklin D. Roosevelt over a third term.

The sugar rationing of World War II could have brought the entire cola industry to its knees, but Mr. Farley's political connections helped Coke escape the rationing. Coke was declared a war priority item, and at the end of the war Coke had 64 bottling plants built around the world — all at the government's expense.

Pepsi retaliated by forming a political alliance of its own, with a little known junior Senator from Wisconsin, Joseph McCarthy. In a battle that foreshadowed his later anti-Communist crusade, he fought for an end to rationing. His usefulness came to an end, however, when it was revealed that Pepsi's Washington representative had given him $20 000.

Pepsi soon forged a more successful political alliance, with Richard Nixon, who was then Vice President. Thanks to some pushing by Pepsi's chairman, Donald Kendall, Pepsi was the only soft drink represented at the American International Exposition. Mr Nixon even got Mr Khrushchev to drink some Pepsi — an event seen by millions.

When Mr Nixon's political career faltered in the early 1960's, Mr Kendall hired him as an international ambassador for Pepsico. Then, as Mr Nixon gained momentum in the late 1960's, Pepsi sales went right along with him. In 1968, when the Democrats lost the presidency, Pepsi machines were installed in the White House cafeteria. In 1971, Mr Nixon sent Mr Kendall to Moscow, and Pepsi became the first U.S. consumer product sold in the Soviet Union.

Meanwhile, Coca-Cola, based in Atlanta, was looking for another Democrat to support. It found a hometown boy. During Jimmy Carter's long march to the White House, he used Coca-Cola money, Coca-Cola jets and Coca-Cola's advertising company. When he was elected, the Pepsi machines in the White House were replaced by Coke machines. Coke also used its Carter connections to take China, just as Pepsi breezed into the Soviet Union with Mr Nixon.

Vocabulary

soda pop (AmE)	a sweet drink containing a harmless gas; soft drink	(süßer) Sprudel
twist	unexpected change or development	Drehung, Wendung
hoopla	shouts of excitement	Rummel, Geschrei
to escalate	to spread and get more serious	eskalieren
implication	being connected with	Verwicklung
sth. is not coincidence	not happening by chance	etwas ist kein Zufall
New Deal	—	Wirtschafts- und Sozialpolitik des Präsidenten Roosevelt
connection	here: (business) relationship	(geschäftliche) Beziehung, Verbindung
war priority item	goods excluded from rationing restrictions during World War II	kriegswichtiger Artikel
to retaliate	to pay back (evil with evil)	Vergeltung üben
crusade	here: struggle for the defence or advance of an idea, opinion, etc.	Kreuzzug
to falter	to lose strength, to weaken	schwächer werden
(to gain) momentum	to gain force by the development of events	Wucht, Schwungkraft
to breeze (into)	to move swiftly and unceremoniously	hereinfegen (wie der Wind), hereinschneien

140

Coca Cola gibt der Verknüpfung zwischen Politik und Limonade eine neue Wendung

Bei all dem Geschrei um den immer heftiger werdenden Krieg um Cola-limonaden wird ein Thema übergangen: die politischen Verknüpfungen.

Wie bei den politischen Parteien gibt es nur zwei bedeutende Gegner: Coca Cola, das Getränk der Demokraten, und Pepsi Cola, die Erfrischung der Republikaner. Gewiß gibt es auch Cola-Getränke für eine dritte Partei, aber ebenso wie in der Politik wird über sie nicht viel geredet.

Diese Verknüpfung zwischen Limonaden und Politik ist kein Zufall. Coca Cola ist unbestritten das Getränk der Mehrheit seit dem New Deal. Die Verbindung zwischen Coca Cola und Politik kam 1932 zustande, als der Vorsitzende der Demokraten, der Postminister James Farley, die Regierungsgeschäfte aufgab, um Vorsitzender der Coca Cola Export Gesellschaft zu werden. Er hatte sich mit Franklin D. Roosevelt wegen einer dritten Amtsperiode entzweit.

Die Rationierung des Zuckers im Zweiten Weltkrieg hätte beinahe die gesamte Cola-Industrie zusammenbrechen lassen, aber Farleys politische Verbindungen halfen Coca Cola, von der Rationierung verschont zu bleiben. Coke wurde zum kriegswichtigen Artikel erklärt, und bis zum Ende des Krieges hatte Coke 64 Abfüllstationen in der ganzen Welt bauen lassen, alle auf Kosten der Regierung.

Pepsi schlug zurück, indem es selbst ein politisches Bündnis mit einem wenig bekannten Senator aus Wisconsin schloß, mit Joseph McCarthy. In einer Schlacht, die seinen späteren antikommunistischen Kreuzzug bereits ahnen ließ, kämpfte er für die Aufhebung der Zuckerrationierung. Als jedoch herauskam, daß ihm der Pepsi-Cola-Vertreter in Washington 20 000 Dollar gegeben hatte, war es vorbei mit McCarthy's guten Diensten.

Pepsi schloß bald darauf ein erfolgreicheres politisches Bündnis mit Richard Nixon, der damals Vizepräsident war. Dank des sanften Druckes durch den Vorsitzenden von Pepsi Cola, Donald Kendall, war Pepsi das einzige alkoholfreie Getränk, das es auf der Internationalen Ausstellung der USA gab. Nixon brachte sogar Chruschtschow dazu, ein wenig Pepsi zu trinken, ein Ereignis, das von Millionen Menschen gesehen wurde.

Während sich Nixons politische Karriere Anfang der sechziger Jahre verzögerte, warb ihn Kendall als international obersten Vertreter für Pepsi Cola. Als Nixon dann in den späten sechziger Jahren an Bedeutung gewann, stiegen die Verkaufszahlen von Pepsi in gleichem Maß. Als die Demokraten 1968 die Präsidentschaft verloren, wurden in der Cafeteria des Weißen Hauses Pepsi-Automaten aufgestellt. 1971 sandte Nixon Kendall nach Moskau, und Pepsi wurde zum ersten Konsumartikel, der in der Sowjetunion verkauft wurde.

In der Zwischenzeit suchte Coca Cola, das seinen Sitz in Atlanta hat, einen anderen Demokraten zur Unterstützung. Es fand einen Einheimischen. Jimmy Carter bediente sich auf seinem langen Weg zum Weißen Haus des Geldes, der Düsenjets und der Werbefirma von Coca Cola. Als er gewählt wurde, tauschte man die Pepsi-Automaten im Weißen Haus gegen Cola-Automaten aus. Um China als Markt zu gewinnen, nützte Coca Cola seine Verbindung zu Carter in der gleichen Weise, wie Pepsi mit Nixon die So — wjetunion als Markt erobert hatte.

142

Polish up your grammar

1. Adjectives or adverbs

Use an adverb if the action is qualified:

They considered this problem thoroughly.

Use an adjective if the subject or object is qualified:

They considered the new Coke good.

Use adjectives with the following verbs:

Coke **tastes** delicious.
That **sounds** fantastic.
He **grew** impatient.
She **seems** happy.
You **look** good in your new dress.

He **became** angry.
They **get** nervous.
It **smells** good.
I **feel** hungry.

2. Conditional sentences

Type I: If they **give** up the old coke   there **will be** a rebellion.

            present tense   future

Type II: If they **gave** up the old Coke   there **would be** a rebellion.

            past tense   conditional

Type III: If they **had given** up . . .   there **would have been** . . .

            past perfect   past conditional